Building Business Apps in C A Step-by-Step Guide to Enterprise Application Development

Américo Moreira

Published by Américo Moreira, 2023.

BUILDING BUSINESS APPS IN C A STEP-BY-STEP GUIDE TO ENTERPRISE APPLICATION DEVELOPMENT

First edition. December 4, 2023.

ISBN: 979-8223618140

Written by Américo Moreira.

Building Business Apps in C

A Step-by-Step Guide to Enterprise Application Development

Américo Moreira

1

1 - Introduction to Building Business Apps in C# and .NET

1.1 Understanding the Importance of Building Business Apps

In today's digital age, businesses rely heavily on technology to streamline their operations, improve efficiency, and gain a competitive edge. Building business applications has become a crucial aspect of modern enterprises, enabling them to automate processes, manage data effectively, and provide valuable insights for decision-making. This section will delve into the importance of building business apps and how they can benefit organizations.

1.1.1 Streamlining Operations and Increasing Efficiency

One of the primary reasons for building business apps is to streamline operations and increase efficiency within an organization. By automating manual processes and integrating various systems, businesses can eliminate repetitive tasks, reduce human errors, and optimize resource utilization. For example, an order processing system can automate the entire order fulfillment process, from capturing customer details to generating invoices and tracking shipments. This automation not only saves time but also ensures accuracy and consistency in the workflow.

1.1.2 Enhancing Data Management and Decision-Making

Data is a valuable asset for any business, and effective data management is crucial for making informed decisions. Building business apps allows organizations to collect, store, and analyze data in a structured manner.

With the right data models and architecture in place, businesses can gain insights into customer behavior, market trends, and operational performance. These insights can drive strategic decision-making, identify areas for improvement, and uncover new business opportunities. For instance, an inventory management system can provide real-time visibility into stock levels, enabling businesses to optimize inventory, reduce costs, and meet customer demands efficiently.

1.1.3 Improving Customer Experience and Satisfaction

In today's competitive market, providing exceptional customer experience is paramount for business success. Building business apps enables organizations to create user-friendly interfaces and personalized experiences for their customers. With well-designed user interfaces, businesses can enhance the ease of use, accessibility, and responsiveness of their applications. For example, a customer relationship management (CRM) system can provide a centralized platform for managing customer interactions, tracking sales leads, and delivering personalized marketing campaigns. This level of customer-centricity can lead to increased customer satisfaction, loyalty, and ultimately, business growth.

1.1.4 Enabling Scalability and Adaptability

As businesses grow and evolve, their requirements change, and they need applications that can scale and adapt accordingly. Building business apps using technologies like C# and .NET provides organizations with the flexibility to accommodate future growth and changing business needs. These technologies offer robust frameworks, libraries, and tools that support scalability, allowing businesses to handle increased data volumes, user traffic, and system complexity. Additionally, the modular nature of C# and .NET enables organizations to add new features, integrate with external systems, and extend functionality without disrupting the existing application.

1.1.5 Gaining a Competitive Edge

In today's competitive landscape, businesses need to differentiate themselves from their competitors. Building custom business apps tailored to specific industry requirements can give organizations a competitive edge. These apps can incorporate industry-specific functionalities, workflows, and business rules, providing a unique value proposition to customers. For example, a healthcare management system can include features like patient records management, appointment scheduling, and medical billing, catering specifically to the needs of healthcare providers. By offering specialized solutions, businesses can attract more customers, increase market share, and establish themselves as industry leaders.

1.1.6 Ensuring Security and Compliance

Data security and compliance are critical considerations for businesses, especially when dealing with sensitive customer information or industry-specific regulations. Building business apps allows organizations to implement robust security measures and ensure compliance with data protection standards. With features like user authentication, role-based access control, and data encryption, businesses can safeguard sensitive data from unauthorized access and protect against security breaches. Moreover, building apps in compliance with industry regulations and standards helps businesses avoid legal and financial repercussions.

In conclusion, building business apps in C# and .NET is essential for organizations looking to streamline operations, enhance data management, improve customer experience, and gain a competitive edge. These apps enable businesses to automate processes, make informed decisions, and adapt to changing requirements. By leveraging the power of technology, businesses can achieve efficiency, scalability, and security while delivering value to their customers and driving business growth. In the following sections, we will explore the fundamentals of C# and .NET framework, planning data models and architecture, designing user interfaces, and other key aspects of building business apps.

1.2 Overview of C# and .NET Framework

In order to build business applications in C# and .NET, it is essential to have a solid understanding of the C# programming language and the .NET Framework. This section will provide an overview of these key components, highlighting their importance and explaining how they work together to enable the development of robust and scalable enterprise applications.

1.2.1 Introduction to C#

C# (pronounced as "C sharp") is a modern, object-oriented programming language developed by Microsoft. It is widely used for building a variety of applications, including desktop, web, and mobile applications. C# is known for its simplicity, readability, and strong type-safety, making it an ideal choice for developing business applications.

C# is part of the .NET ecosystem, which provides a rich set of libraries and tools for application development. It is a statically-typed language, meaning that variables must be declared with their types at compile-time. This helps catch errors early and improves code reliability.

1.2.2 Introduction to the .NET Framework

The .NET Framework is a software development platform created by Microsoft. It provides a runtime environment for executing applications and a set of libraries and tools for building various types of applications. The .NET Framework supports multiple programming languages, including C#, Visual Basic, and F#.

The key components of the .NET Framework include:

Common Language Runtime (CLR)

The Common Language Runtime (CLR) is the execution engine of the .NET Framework. It provides services such as memory management, exception handling, and security. The CLR compiles C# code into an intermediate language called Common Intermediate Language (CIL), which is then executed by the runtime.

Base Class Library (BCL)

The Base Class Library (BCL) is a collection of classes and types that provide a wide range of functionality for building applications. It includes classes for working with strings, collections, file I/O, networking, and much more. The BCL simplifies common programming tasks and allows developers to focus on application-specific logic.

Language Integrated Query (LINQ)

Language Integrated Query (LINQ) is a powerful feature of C# and the .NET Framework that allows developers to query and manipulate data from various sources, such as databases, XML, and collections. LINQ provides a unified syntax for querying different data sources, making it easier to work with data in a consistent and efficient manner.

Windows Presentation Foundation (WPF)

Windows Presentation Foundation (WPF) is a UI framework for building desktop applications with rich user interfaces. It provides a flexible and powerful model for creating visually appealing and interactive applications. WPF uses XAML (eXtensible Application Markup Language) to define the UI layout and behavior, allowing for a clear separation between the UI and the application logic.

ASP.NET

ASP.NET is a web development framework that allows developers to build dynamic and scalable web applications. It provides a model-view-controller (MVC) architecture for organizing code and a rich set of controls and components for creating web UIs. ASP.NET supports various web technologies, such as HTML, CSS, JavaScript, and AJAX, making it a versatile platform for building modern web applications.

1.2.3 Benefits of C# and .NET for Business Application Development

The combination of C# and the .NET Framework offers several benefits for building business applications:

Productivity and Efficiency

C# is a high-level language that provides a clean and expressive syntax, allowing developers to write code quickly and efficiently. The .NET Framework provides a rich set of libraries and tools that simplify common programming tasks, reducing development time and effort.

Scalability and Performance

The .NET Framework is designed to support the development of scalable and high-performance applications. It provides features such as just-in-time (JIT) compilation, garbage collection, and multi-threading support, which help optimize application performance and resource utilization.

Security and Reliability

C# and the .NET Framework have built-in security features that help protect applications from common security threats, such as SQL injection and cross-site scripting (XSS). The CLR enforces type-safety and provides mechanisms for handling exceptions, ensuring that applications are robust and reliable.

Integration and Interoperability

The .NET Framework supports seamless integration with other technologies and systems. It provides libraries for working with databases, web services, messaging systems, and more. Additionally, C# can interoperate with existing code written in other languages, such as C++ and COM, allowing for easy integration with legacy systems.

In conclusion, C# and the .NET Framework provide a powerful and versatile platform for building business applications. Their simplicity, productivity, scalability, and security features make them an ideal choice for developing enterprise-grade applications. In the next sections of this book, we will dive deeper into the various aspects of building business apps in C# and .NET, exploring topics such as data modeling, UI design, database integration, security, and more.

1.3 Planning Data Models and Architecture

In order to build a successful business application, it is crucial to start with a solid foundation. This foundation includes planning the data models and architecture of your application. By carefully considering these aspects, you can ensure that your application is efficient, scalable, and meets the needs of your business.

1.3.1 Understanding the Importance of Data Models

Data models serve as the blueprint for your application's data structure. They define how data is organized, stored, and accessed within your application. A well-designed data model is essential for ensuring data integrity, consistency, and efficiency.

When planning your data models, it is important to consider the specific requirements of your business. This includes understanding the types of data that need to be stored, the relationships between different data entities, and the operations that will be performed on the data.

1.3.2 Identifying Data Entities and Relationships

The first step in planning your data models is to identify the different data entities that will be part of your application. Data entities represent the different objects or concepts that your application will work with. For example, in an inventory management system, data entities may include products, orders, and customers.

Once you have identified the data entities, you need to determine the relationships between them. Relationships define how the data entities are connected or associated with each other. Common types of relationships include one-to-one, one-to-many, and many-to-many relationships.

Understanding the relationships between data entities is crucial for designing an efficient and effective data model. It helps ensure that data is stored and retrieved in a way that accurately represents the real-world relationships between objects.

1.3.3 Designing the Data Model

With a clear understanding of the data entities and relationships, you can now start designing the data model for your application. The data model defines the structure and organization of the data within your application.

When designing the data model, you need to consider factors such as data types, constraints, and indexing. Data types define the format and size of the data that can be stored in each field. Constraints ensure that the data meets certain rules or conditions. Indexing improves the performance of data retrieval operations by creating efficient data access paths.

It is also important to consider the scalability and performance requirements of your application when designing the data model. This includes considering factors such as data partitioning, caching, and optimization techniques.

1.3.4 Choosing the Right Architecture

In addition to planning the data models, it is equally important to consider the overall architecture of your application. The architecture defines how different components of your application interact with each other and how the application as a whole is structured.

There are various architectural patterns that can be used for building business applications, such as the layered architecture, the client-server architecture, and the microservices architecture. Each architecture has its own advantages and considerations, and the choice depends on factors such as the complexity of the application, scalability requirements, and integration needs.

When choosing the architecture, it is important to consider factors such as modularity, maintainability, and extensibility. A well-designed architecture allows for easy integration of new features, scalability to handle increasing data and user loads, and flexibility to adapt to changing business requirements.

1.3.5 Documenting the Data Models and Architecture

Once you have planned your data models and architecture, it is important to document them. Documentation serves as a reference for developers, stakeholders, and future maintainers of the application.

The documentation should include detailed descriptions of the data models, including the entities, relationships, and attributes. It should also include diagrams, such as entity-relationship diagrams or class diagrams, to visually represent the data models and architecture.

By documenting the data models and architecture, you ensure that everyone involved in the development process has a clear understanding of how the application is structured and how the data is organized. This helps prevent misunderstandings, reduces development time, and facilitates future enhancements or modifications to the application.

Conclusion

Planning the data models and architecture of your business application is a critical step in the development process. It lays the foundation for a well-structured, efficient, and scalable application. By carefully considering the data entities, relationships, and overall architecture, you can ensure that your application meets the specific needs of your business and provides a solid platform for future growth and enhancements.

1.4 Designing User Interfaces with Windows Forms

User interfaces play a crucial role in the success of any business application. They are the bridge between the user and the underlying functionality of the application. In this section, we will explore the process of designing user interfaces using Windows Forms, a powerful framework provided by Microsoft for building desktop applications in C# and .NET.

1.4.1 Introduction to Windows Forms

Windows Forms is a graphical user interface (GUI) framework that allows developers to create rich and interactive desktop applications. It provides a wide range of controls and components that can be used to design intuitive and visually appealing user interfaces. With Windows Forms, you can create windows, dialog boxes, menus, buttons, text boxes, and many other elements that make up the user interface of an application.

1.4.2 Getting Started with Windows Forms

To start designing user interfaces with Windows Forms, you need to have a basic understanding of the framework and its components. The main building block of a Windows Forms application is the Form class, which represents a window or a dialog box. You can add controls to a form by dragging and dropping them from the Visual Studio Toolbox, which contains a wide range of pre-built controls.

Once you have added controls to a form, you can customize their properties, such as size, position, color, font, and behavior. You can also handle events raised by the controls, such as button clicks or text changes, to add interactivity to your application.

1.4.3 Layout and Design Principles

When designing user interfaces, it is important to consider the layout and design principles to ensure a visually appealing and user-friendly application. Here are some key principles to keep in mind:

1.4.3.1 Consistency

Maintaining consistency throughout the application helps users understand and navigate the interface more easily. Use consistent colors, fonts, and styles across different screens and controls. This creates a sense of familiarity and reduces cognitive load for the users.

1.4.3.2 Simplicity

Keep the user interface simple and intuitive. Avoid cluttering the screen with too many controls or information. Use clear and concise labels, and organize controls in a logical and easy-to-understand manner. Remember, simplicity enhances usability.

1.4.3.3 Responsiveness

Design your user interface to be responsive and provide immediate feedback to user actions. For example, when a button is clicked, provide visual feedback such as highlighting or disabling the button to indicate that the action is being processed. This helps users understand that their actions are being recognized by the application.

1.4.3.4 Accessibility

Consider the needs of users with disabilities when designing your user interface. Ensure that your application is accessible to users with visual impairments, hearing impairments, or motor disabilities. Provide alternative text for images, support keyboard navigation, and use color schemes that are accessible to color-blind users.

1.4.4 Controls and Components

Windows Forms provides a wide range of controls and components that can be used to build the user interface of your application. Here are some commonly used controls:

1.4.4.1 Labels

Labels are used to display text or images on the screen. They are typically used to provide instructions or descriptions for other controls.

1.4.4.2 Text Boxes

Text boxes allow users to input and edit text. They are commonly used for data entry or search functionality.

1.4.4.3 Buttons

Buttons are used to trigger actions or submit forms. They can have different styles, such as standard buttons, check boxes, or radio buttons.

1.4.4.4 List Boxes and Combo Boxes

List boxes and combo boxes are used to display a list of options from which the user can select. List boxes allow multiple selections, while combo boxes allow a single selection.

1.4.4.5 Data Grid View

The Data Grid View control is used to display and edit tabular data. It provides features such as sorting, filtering, and data binding.

1.4.4.6 Menu Strips and Tool Strips

Menu strips and tool strips are used to create menus and toolbars in your application. They provide a convenient way to organize and access different functionalities.

1.4.5 Event Handling

Event handling is an essential part of designing user interfaces. Events are actions or occurrences that happen in the application, such as button clicks or mouse movements. By handling events, you can add interactivity to your application and respond to user actions.

In Windows Forms, you can handle events by writing event handlers, which are methods that are executed when a specific event occurs. Event handlers are associated with controls and are triggered when the corresponding event is raised.

1.4.6 Visual Studio Designer

Visual Studio provides a powerful designer tool that makes it easy to design user interfaces using Windows Forms. The designer allows you to visually create and customize forms, add controls, set properties, and handle events. It provides a drag-and-drop interface, making it intuitive and efficient to design your application's user interface.

1.4.7 Best Practices for User Interface Design

When designing user interfaces with Windows Forms, it is important to follow best practices to ensure a high-quality and user-friendly application. Here are some best practices to consider:

- Use consistent naming conventions for controls and variables.
- Group related controls together to improve usability.
- Provide meaningful error messages and validation feedback.
- Use appropriate control sizes and spacing to enhance readability.
- Test your user interface on different screen resolutions and devices to ensure responsiveness.

By following these best practices, you can create user interfaces that are intuitive, visually appealing, and enhance the overall user experience of your business application.

In the next chapter, we will explore working with databases and ORM frameworks to store and retrieve data in our business application.

2 - Working with Databases and ORM Frameworks

2.1 Introduction to SQL Server Databases

In the world of enterprise application development, databases play a crucial role in storing and managing data. SQL Server, a relational database management system developed by Microsoft, is widely used in the industry due to its robustness, scalability, and security features. In this section, we will explore the fundamentals of SQL Server databases and how they can be leveraged in building business applications using C# and .NET.

2.1.1 Understanding Relational Databases

Before diving into SQL Server specifically, it is important to understand the concept of relational databases. A relational database organizes data into tables, where each table consists of rows and columns. These tables are related to each other through defined relationships, allowing for efficient data retrieval and manipulation.

Relational databases provide a structured approach to data management, ensuring data integrity and consistency. They offer a wide range of features such as data indexing, transaction management, and query optimization, making them suitable for handling complex business scenarios.

2.1.2 Overview of SQL Server

SQL Server is a powerful and feature-rich relational database management system that provides a comprehensive set of tools and services for building and managing databases. It offers various editions, including the Express, Standard, and Enterprise editions, catering to different application requirements and budgets.

SQL Server supports the SQL (Structured Query Language) standard, which is a language used to interact with relational databases. With SQL, developers can perform operations such as creating and modifying database objects, querying data, and managing security.

2.1.3 Benefits of SQL Server for Business Apps

When it comes to building business applications, SQL Server offers several advantages that make it a popular choice among developers:

1. **Scalability**: SQL Server is designed to handle large amounts of data and high user concurrency. It provides features like partitioning, replication, and clustering to ensure optimal performance and scalability.
2. **Security**: SQL Server offers robust security features to protect sensitive business data. It supports authentication mechanisms, role-based access control, and encryption to safeguard against unauthorized access.
3. **Integration**: SQL Server seamlessly integrates with other Microsoft technologies, such as .NET Framework and Visual Studio. This integration allows for efficient development, debugging, and deployment of database-driven applications.
4. **Performance Optimization**: SQL Server provides tools and techniques to optimize query performance, such as query execution plans, indexing, and statistics. These features help developers fine-tune their applications for optimal speed and efficiency.

2.1.4 SQL Server Tools and Services

To work with SQL Server effectively, developers can leverage a range of tools and services provided by Microsoft:

1. **SQL Server Management Studio (SSMS)**: SSMS is a

graphical user interface tool that allows developers to manage and administer SQL Server databases. It provides features for creating and modifying database objects, writing and executing queries, and monitoring server performance.

2. **SQL Server Data Tools (SSDT)**: SSDT is an integrated development environment (IDE) for building and deploying SQL Server databases. It provides a rich set of features for designing database schemas, writing stored procedures, and generating deployment scripts.

3. **Entity Framework (EF)**: EF is an object-relational mapping (ORM) framework that simplifies database access and manipulation in .NET applications. It provides a higher-level abstraction over SQL Server databases, allowing developers to work with entities and relationships instead of writing raw SQL queries.

Conclusion

In this section, we have introduced SQL Server databases and their significance in building business applications. We have explored the benefits of SQL Server, including scalability, security, integration, and performance optimization. Additionally, we have highlighted the tools and services provided by Microsoft to facilitate efficient database development and management.

In the next section, we will delve deeper into creating and managing databases in SQL Server, laying the foundation for building robust and scalable business applications.

2.2 Creating and Managing Databases

In order to build robust and scalable business applications, it is crucial to have a solid foundation in database management. This includes creating and managing databases efficiently. In this section, we will explore the step-by-step process of creating and managing databases using SQL Server, one of the most popular database management systems in the industry.

2.2.1 Understanding the Importance of Databases

Databases play a vital role in business applications as they serve as the backbone for storing and retrieving data. They provide a structured and organized way to manage and manipulate data, ensuring data integrity and consistency. By creating and managing databases effectively, you can ensure that your business applications have a reliable and efficient data storage system.

2.2.2 Choosing the Right Database Management System

Before diving into the process of creating and managing databases, it is essential to choose the right database management system (DBMS) for your business application. SQL Server is a popular choice due to its robustness, scalability, and extensive features. However, other DBMS options like MySQL, Oracle, or PostgreSQL may also be suitable depending on your specific requirements.

2.2.3 Creating a Database

To create a database in SQL Server, follow these steps:

1. Open SQL Server Management Studio (SSMS), which is a graphical tool for managing SQL Server databases.

2. Connect to the SQL Server instance where you want to create the database.
3. Right-click on the "Databases" folder in the Object Explorer pane and select "New Database."
4. In the "New Database" dialog, provide a name for the database and specify the initial size and growth options.
5. Click "OK" to create the database.

2.2.4 Managing Database Objects

Once the database is created, you can start managing its objects such as tables, views, stored procedures, and functions. These objects define the structure and behavior of the data within the database.

2.2.4.1 Creating Tables

Tables are used to store data in a structured manner. To create a table, you need to define its columns and specify the data types and constraints for each column. Here's an example of creating a "Customers" table:

```
CREATE TABLE Customers (
CustomerId INT PRIMARY KEY,
FirstName VARCHAR(50) NOT NULL,
LastName VARCHAR(50) NOT NULL,
Email VARCHAR(100) UNIQUE,
BirthDate DATE
);
```

2.2.4.2 Creating Views

Views provide a way to present data from one or more tables in a customized manner. They can simplify complex queries and provide a simplified interface for accessing data. To create a view, you need to define the query that retrieves the desired data. Here's an example of creating a "CustomersView" that retrieves customer details:

```
CREATE VIEW CustomersView AS
SELECT CustomerId, FirstName, LastName, Email
FROM Customers;
```

2.2.4.3 Creating Stored Procedures

Stored procedures are precompiled sets of SQL statements that can be executed repeatedly. They are used to encapsulate business logic and provide a secure and efficient way to interact with the database. To create a stored procedure, you need to define the SQL statements and parameters. Here's an example of creating a stored procedure to insert a new customer:

```
CREATE PROCEDURE InsertCustomer
@FirstName VARCHAR(50),
@LastName VARCHAR(50),
@Email VARCHAR(100),
@BirthDate DATE
AS
INSERT INTO Customers (FirstName, LastName, Email, BirthDate)
VALUES (@FirstName, @LastName, @Email, @BirthDate);
```

2.2.4.4 Creating Functions

Functions are similar to stored procedures but return a value. They can be used in SQL queries and provide a way to encapsulate reusable logic. To create a function, you need to define the return type, parameters, and the logic. Here's an example of creating a function to calculate the age of a customer:

```
CREATE FUNCTION CalculateAge
```

```
(@BirthDate DATE)
RETURNS INT
AS
BEGIN
DECLARE @Age INT;
SET @Age = DATEDIFF(YEAR, @BirthDate, GETDATE());
RETURN @Age;
END;
```

2.2.5 Managing Database Security

Database security is a critical aspect of managing databases. It involves controlling access to the database objects and ensuring data confidentiality, integrity, and availability. Here are some key considerations for managing database security:

- Granting appropriate permissions to users and roles.
- Implementing strong passwords and enforcing password policies.
- Encrypting sensitive data to protect it from unauthorized access.
- Regularly auditing and monitoring database activities.
- Applying security patches and updates to the database management system.

2.2.6 Backing Up and Restoring Databases

Regularly backing up databases is essential to protect against data loss and ensure business continuity. SQL Server provides various backup and restore options to create backups and restore them when needed. It is recommended to follow a backup strategy that includes full backups, differential backups, and transaction log backups.

To back up a database, you can use SQL Server Management Studio or execute T-SQL commands. Similarly, to restore a database, you can use the graphical interface or T-SQL commands.

Conclusion

Creating and managing databases is a fundamental aspect of building business applications. By understanding the importance of databases, choosing the right database management system, and following best practices for creating and managing database objects, you can ensure a solid foundation for your business applications. Additionally, managing database security and implementing backup and restore strategies are crucial for data protection and business continuity.

2.3 Working with Entity Framework for Object-Relational Mapping

In modern enterprise application development, working with databases is an essential aspect. The ability to efficiently store, retrieve, and manipulate data is crucial for building robust and scalable business applications. Traditionally, developers had to write complex SQL queries and manage the mapping between the relational database and the application's object model manually. However, with the advent of Object-Relational Mapping (ORM) frameworks, such as Entity Framework, this process has become significantly easier and more efficient.

2.3.1 Introduction to Entity Framework

Entity Framework (EF) is an ORM framework provided by Microsoft as part of the .NET ecosystem. It simplifies the process of working with databases by allowing developers to interact with the database using object-oriented programming concepts. EF provides a set of tools and libraries that enable developers to perform tasks such as database schema creation, data querying, and data manipulation using C# or any other .NET language.

2.3.2 Benefits of Using Entity Framework

Using Entity Framework offers several benefits when working with databases in enterprise applications:

1. **Increased productivity**: Entity Framework eliminates the need for writing complex SQL queries manually. Instead, developers can focus on writing business logic using familiar object-oriented programming techniques, resulting in increased productivity and reduced development time.

2. **Simplified data access**: With Entity Framework, developers can interact with the database using a high-level abstraction layer. This abstraction layer handles the mapping between the database tables and the application's object model, making data access operations more intuitive and less error-prone.

3. **Database independence**: Entity Framework supports multiple database providers, including SQL Server, MySQL, Oracle, and SQLite. This allows developers to switch between different database systems without having to rewrite the data access code.

4. **Automatic change tracking**: Entity Framework tracks changes made to the entities within the application automatically. This feature simplifies the process of persisting changes to the database, as EF can generate the necessary SQL statements to update, insert, or delete records based on the changes detected.

5. **Query optimization**: Entity Framework includes a query optimization engine that translates LINQ (Language Integrated Query) expressions into efficient SQL queries. This ensures that the database queries generated by EF are optimized for performance, resulting in faster data retrieval.

2.3.3 Getting Started with Entity Framework

To start working with Entity Framework, you need to set up your project and configure the necessary dependencies. Follow these steps to get started:

1. **Install Entity Framework**: Entity Framework can be installed using NuGet, the package manager for .NET. Open the NuGet Package Manager Console in Visual Studio and run the following command: Install-Package EntityFramework. This will download and install the latest

version of Entity Framework for your project.

2. **Create a data model**: Define the data model for your application by creating classes that represent the entities in your database. An entity class typically corresponds to a table in the database, and its properties represent the columns of that table. You can use attributes or fluent API to configure the mapping between the entity class and the database table.

3. **Create a DbContext**: The DbContext class is the main entry point for interacting with the database using Entity Framework. It represents a session with the database and provides methods for querying and manipulating data. Create a class that derives from DbContext and define properties for each entity class you want to work with.

4. **Configure the connection string**: Entity Framework requires a connection string to connect to the database. The connection string contains information such as the server name, database name, and authentication credentials. You can configure the connection string in the application's configuration file (e.g., app.config or web.config) or provide it programmatically.

5. **Perform database operations**: Once you have set up the data model, DbContext, and connection string, you can start performing database operations using Entity Framework. This includes querying data using LINQ, inserting, updating, and deleting records, and executing stored procedures.

2.3.4 Advanced Entity Framework Features

Entity Framework provides several advanced features that can further enhance your experience when working with databases:

1. **Code First Migrations**: Entity Framework Code First Migrations allows you to evolve your database schema over

time as your application's requirements change. It enables you to create and apply database schema changes using code-based migrations, ensuring that your database stays in sync with your application's data model.

2. **Database Initialization**: Entity Framework supports different strategies for initializing the database when your application starts. You can choose to create the database if it doesn't exist, drop and recreate the database every time the application starts, or use a custom initialization strategy.

3. **Lazy Loading**: Entity Framework supports lazy loading, which means that related entities are loaded from the database only when accessed for the first time. This can improve performance by reducing the amount of data retrieved from the database initially.

4. **Eager Loading**: In contrast to lazy loading, eager loading allows you to load related entities along with the main entity in a single database query. This can help reduce the number of database round-trips and improve performance when accessing related data.

5. **Transactions**: Entity Framework supports transactions, allowing you to perform multiple database operations as a single atomic unit. This ensures that either all the operations succeed or none of them are applied, maintaining data integrity.

Conclusion

Entity Framework is a powerful ORM framework that simplifies working with databases in enterprise applications. It provides a high-level abstraction layer that allows developers to interact with the database using object-oriented programming concepts. By leveraging Entity Framework, developers can increase productivity, simplify data access, and take advantage of advanced features such as code-first migrations, lazy loading, and transactions. Incorporating Entity Framework into your application development process can significantly streamline the database-related aspects of building business apps in C# and .NET.

2.4 Implementing Data Access Layer

The data access layer is a crucial component of any enterprise application. It is responsible for interacting with the database and retrieving or persisting data. In this section, we will explore the various techniques and best practices for implementing the data access layer in your business applications using C# and .NET.

2.4.1 Choosing the Right Data Access Technology

Before diving into the implementation details, it is essential to choose the right data access technology for your application. In the .NET ecosystem, you have several options, including ADO.NET, Entity Framework, Dapper, and more. Each technology has its strengths and weaknesses, so it's important to consider factors such as performance, ease of use, and maintainability.

ADO.NET

ADO.NET is the traditional data access technology in the .NET framework. It provides a low-level API for interacting with databases, allowing you to write raw SQL queries and execute them against the database. While ADO.NET offers maximum control and performance, it requires more code and can be more error-prone compared to higher-level ORMs.

Entity Framework

Entity Framework (EF) is a popular object-relational mapping (ORM) framework in the .NET ecosystem. It simplifies data access by providing a higher-level abstraction over the database. With EF, you can work with objects and entities instead of writing raw SQL queries. It also supports various database providers, making it easy to switch between different databases.

Dapper

Dapper is a lightweight micro-ORM that focuses on performance and simplicity. It provides a simple API for mapping database results to objects and vice versa. Dapper is known for its speed and efficiency, making it an excellent choice for applications that require high-performance data access.

2.4.2 Creating a Data Access Layer

Once you have chosen the appropriate data access technology, it's time to create the data access layer in your application. The data access layer acts as an intermediary between the business logic layer and the database, encapsulating all the data access operations.

Repository Pattern

One common design pattern used in the data access layer is the repository pattern. The repository pattern provides a standardized way to interact with the database by encapsulating the data access logic within repositories. A repository acts as a collection-like interface for querying and manipulating data.

To implement the repository pattern, you can create a separate class for each entity in your application. Each repository class should provide methods for common data operations such as querying, inserting, updating, and deleting entities.

Example: Implementing a Repository with Entity Framework

Let's take a look at an example of implementing a repository using Entity Framework. Assume we have an application that manages customer data. We can create a CustomerRepository class that encapsulates all the data access operations related to customers.

```
public class CustomerRepository
{
private readonly DbContext _dbContext;
public CustomerRepository(DbContext dbContext)
{
_dbContext = dbContext;
}
public IEnumerable<Customer> GetAllCustomers()
{
return _dbContext.Set<Customer>().ToList();
}
public void AddCustomer(Customer customer)
{
_dbContext.Set<Customer>().Add(customer);
_dbContext.SaveChanges();
}
// Other data access methods...
}
```

In the above example, the CustomerRepository class takes an instance of the DbContext class (provided by Entity Framework) in its constructor. It then exposes methods such as GetAllCustomers and AddCustomer for querying and inserting customers, respectively.

2.4.3 Handling Transactions

In many business applications, it is essential to maintain data consistency and integrity. Transactions provide a way to group multiple database operations into a single atomic unit. If any operation within a transaction fails, all the changes made within that transaction can be rolled back, ensuring data integrity.

TransactionScope

In .NET, you can use the TransactionScope class to manage transactions. The TransactionScope class provides a simple and intuitive API for creating and managing transactions. It automatically enlists all the database operations within its scope into the transaction.

```
using (var scope = new TransactionScope())
{
// Perform database operations within the transaction
scope.Complete(); // Commit the transaction
}
```

In the above example, all the database operations within the TransactionScope will be part of the same transaction. If an exception occurs or the Complete method is not called, the transaction will be rolled back.

2.4.4 Performance Considerations

When implementing the data access layer, it's crucial to consider performance. Here are a few tips to improve the performance of your data access layer:

- Use parameterized queries to prevent SQL injection attacks and improve query execution plan caching.
- Use appropriate indexing on database tables to improve query performance.

- Consider caching frequently accessed data to reduce database round-trips.
- Use asynchronous data access methods to improve scalability and responsiveness.

By following these best practices, you can ensure that your data access layer performs optimally and provides a seamless experience for your users.

Conclusion

In this section, we explored the importance of the data access layer in building business applications. We discussed different data access technologies such as ADO.NET, Entity Framework, and Dapper. We also learned how to implement the data access layer using the repository pattern and handle transactions. Finally, we discussed performance considerations to optimize the data access layer. With this knowledge, you can now confidently implement the data access layer in your own business applications using C# and .NET.

3 - Implementing Business Logic and Validation

3.1 Understanding Business Logic and Validation

In the world of enterprise application development, business logic and validation play a crucial role in ensuring the accuracy, integrity, and reliability of the data and processes within the application. Business logic refers to the rules, algorithms, and workflows that define how the application operates and handles various business scenarios. Validation, on the other hand, involves verifying the correctness and consistency of the data entered by users or received from external sources.

3.1.1 Importance of Business Logic

Business logic forms the backbone of any business application. It encapsulates the core functionality and rules that drive the application's behavior and enable it to automate and streamline business processes. By implementing business logic, you can ensure that the application operates in a consistent and predictable manner, adhering to the specific requirements and regulations of the business domain.

The importance of business logic lies in its ability to:

1. **Enforce Business Rules**: Business rules define the policies, procedures, and constraints that govern how the application should handle various scenarios. By implementing business logic, you can enforce these rules and ensure that the application operates in accordance with the business requirements.

2. **Maintain Data Integrity**: Business logic helps maintain the integrity of the data stored in the application's database. It

ensures that the data is accurate, consistent, and valid by performing necessary checks, calculations, and validations before storing or manipulating the data.

3. **Enable Workflow Automation**: Business logic enables the automation of complex business workflows and processes. By defining the sequence of steps, conditions, and actions, you can streamline and automate repetitive tasks, reducing manual effort and improving efficiency.

4. **Support Decision-Making**: Business logic provides the foundation for making informed decisions within the application. By incorporating decision-making algorithms and rules, you can enable the application to analyze data, evaluate conditions, and generate meaningful insights to support decision-making processes.

3.1.2 Types of Business Logic

Business logic can be categorized into two main types: **client-side** and **server-side** logic.

1. **Client-side Logic**: Client-side logic runs on the user's device, typically within the user interface layer of the application. It is responsible for handling user interactions, input validation, and immediate feedback. Client-side logic is often implemented using JavaScript or other client-side scripting languages. It helps improve the user experience by providing real-time validation and feedback without the need for server round-trips.

2. **Server-side Logic**: Server-side logic runs on the application server and is responsible for processing requests, executing business rules, and interacting with the database. It ensures the consistency and integrity of the data by performing server-side validations, calculations, and complex business operations.

Server-side logic is implemented using programming languages like C# and is executed on the server before sending the response back to the client.

3.1.3 Implementing Business Validation

Validation is a critical aspect of building business applications. It ensures that the data entered by users or received from external sources is accurate, consistent, and valid. By implementing validation, you can prevent data corruption, improve data quality, and enhance the overall reliability of the application.

When implementing business validation, consider the following:

1. **Data Type Validation**: Validate that the data entered by users matches the expected data type. For example, ensure that a numeric field only accepts numbers, a date field only accepts valid dates, and a text field does not exceed the maximum allowed length.

2. **Range and Constraint Validation**: Validate that the data falls within the acceptable range or meets specific constraints. For example, ensure that a numeric field falls within a specified range, a date is within a valid period, or a text field does not contain prohibited characters.

3. **Business Rule Validation**: Validate that the data adheres to the defined business rules and policies. For example, ensure that a discount percentage is within the allowed range, a product quantity does not exceed the available stock, or a customer's credit limit is not exceeded.

4. **Cross-Field Validation**: Validate the relationship and consistency between multiple fields. For example, ensure that the start date of an event is before the end date, the total quantity of items in an order matches the sum of individual quantities, or the selected options in a form do not conflict

with each other.

5. **Custom Validation**: Implement custom validation rules specific to your business requirements. This may involve complex calculations, external service integrations, or data lookups. Custom validation allows you to enforce unique business rules that are not covered by standard validation techniques.

To implement validation in your C# application, you can leverage the built-in validation features provided by the .NET framework, such as data annotations, validation attributes, and validation rules. These features allow you to declaratively define validation rules and apply them to your data models or user interface elements.

Additionally, you can implement custom validation logic by writing custom validation methods or by utilizing third-party validation libraries. These libraries provide advanced validation capabilities and allow you to handle complex validation scenarios with ease.

By implementing robust business logic and validation in your C# and .NET applications, you can ensure the accuracy, reliability, and integrity of your data and processes. This, in turn, leads to more efficient and effective business operations, improved user experience, and increased customer satisfaction.

3.2 Implementing Business Rules and Workflows

In any business application, it is crucial to implement business rules and workflows to ensure that the application operates according to the specific requirements and processes of the organization. Business rules define the logic and constraints that govern the behavior of the application, while workflows define the sequence of activities and tasks that need to be performed to accomplish a specific business process. In this section, we will explore how to implement business rules and workflows in C# and .NET.

3.2.1 Defining Business Rules

Before implementing business rules, it is essential to have a clear understanding of the specific rules that need to be enforced in the application. These rules can vary depending on the nature of the business and the requirements of the application. Some common examples of business rules include:

- Validation rules: These rules ensure that the data entered by the user is valid and meets the specified criteria. For example, validating that a date falls within a certain range or that a numeric value is within acceptable limits.
- Calculation rules: These rules perform calculations based on the input data and generate the desired output. For example, calculating the total cost of an order based on the quantity and unit price.
- Authorization rules: These rules determine the access rights and permissions of users based on their roles and responsibilities. For example, allowing only managers to approve certain actions or restricting access to sensitive data.

To implement business rules in C# and .NET, you can leverage various techniques and frameworks. One common approach is to use a rules engine, which provides a flexible and configurable way to define and execute business rules. The .NET ecosystem offers several rules engine libraries, such as NRules and Drools.NET, that can be integrated into your application.

3.2.2 Implementing Workflows

Workflows define the sequence of activities and tasks that need to be performed to accomplish a specific business process. They provide a visual representation of the steps involved and the conditions that determine the flow of execution. In C# and .NET, you can implement workflows using the Windows Workflow Foundation (WF) framework.

Windows Workflow Foundation is a powerful framework that allows you to design, execute, and manage workflows in your application. It provides a visual designer, called the Workflow Designer, which allows you to create workflows by dragging and dropping activities onto a canvas and defining the connections between them. Activities represent individual steps or tasks in the workflow, and they can be customized to perform specific actions.

To implement workflows using Windows Workflow Foundation, you need to follow these steps:

1. Define the workflow structure: Start by identifying the activities and their relationships that make up the workflow. Determine the conditions that determine the flow of execution between activities.

2. Design the workflow using the Workflow Designer: Open the Workflow Designer and create a new workflow. Drag and drop activities onto the canvas and connect them to define the flow of execution. Configure the properties of each activity to

specify its behavior.

3. Implement custom activities: If the built-in activities provided by Windows Workflow Foundation do not meet your requirements, you can create custom activities by deriving from the Activity base class. Implement the necessary logic and behavior in these custom activities.

4. Integrate the workflow into your application: Once the workflow is designed and implemented, you need to integrate it into your application. This involves creating an instance of the workflow, setting any required input parameters, and starting the execution. You can also handle events and monitor the progress of the workflow.

Windows Workflow Foundation provides a rich set of features and capabilities for implementing complex workflows. It supports features like persistence, compensation, and error handling, which are essential for building robust and reliable workflows.

3.2.3 Testing and Validating Business Rules and Workflows

Testing and validating business rules and workflows are crucial to ensure that they function correctly and meet the desired requirements. In C# and .NET, you can use various testing frameworks and techniques to test your business rules and workflows.

For testing business rules, you can write unit tests that validate the behavior of individual rules. You can use testing frameworks like NUnit or MSTest to write these tests. By providing different input values and asserting the expected output, you can verify that the rules are working as expected.

When it comes to testing workflows, you can write integration tests that simulate the execution of the workflow and validate its behavior. You can use frameworks like SpecFlow or xUnit to write these tests.

By defining test scenarios and executing the workflow with different inputs, you can ensure that the workflow follows the correct sequence of activities and produces the expected results.

In addition to testing, it is also essential to validate the business rules and workflows during the development process. This can be done by conducting code reviews, peer reviews, and walkthroughs to identify any potential issues or inconsistencies. It is also beneficial to involve domain experts and stakeholders in the validation process to ensure that the rules and workflows align with the business requirements.

By implementing and testing business rules and workflows effectively, you can ensure that your application operates according to the specific requirements and processes of the organization. This will result in a more robust and reliable business application that meets the needs of the users and stakeholders.

3.3 Validating User Input

User input validation is a crucial aspect of building business applications. It ensures that the data entered by users is accurate, complete, and meets the required criteria. By validating user input, you can prevent errors, improve data integrity, and enhance the overall user experience. In this section, we will explore various techniques and best practices for validating user input in C# and .NET.

3.3.1 Importance of User Input Validation

Validating user input is essential for several reasons. Firstly, it helps maintain data integrity by ensuring that only valid and expected values are accepted. This prevents the application from storing incorrect or inconsistent data, which can lead to issues down the line. Secondly, it enhances the user experience by providing immediate feedback to users when they enter invalid data. This feedback can be in the form of error messages, highlighting the incorrect fields, or suggesting valid alternatives. Lastly, user input validation plays a crucial role in preventing security vulnerabilities such as SQL injection, cross-site scripting (XSS), and other types of attacks.

3.3.2 Types of User Input Validation

There are various types of user input validation techniques that you can employ in your business applications. Let's explore some of the most common ones:

3.3.2.1 Required Fields Validation

One of the simplest forms of validation is to ensure that required fields are not left empty. This validation ensures that users provide essential information before proceeding. You can achieve this by checking if the input fields have values and displaying an error message if they are empty.

3.3.2.2 Data Type Validation

Data type validation ensures that the entered data matches the expected data type. For example, if a field expects a numeric value, you can validate whether the input is a valid number. Similarly, if a field expects a date, you can validate whether the input is a valid date format. By enforcing data type validation, you can prevent data inconsistencies and errors.

3.3.2.3 Length and Format Validation

Length and format validation ensure that the entered data meets specific criteria in terms of length and format. For example, you can validate that a password field has a minimum length and contains a combination of uppercase and lowercase letters, numbers, and special characters. Similarly, you can validate that an email address field follows a valid email format. By enforcing length and format validation, you can ensure that the entered data meets the required standards.

3.3.2.4 Range and Boundary Validation

Range and boundary validation ensure that the entered data falls within a specific range or boundary. For example, if a field expects a numeric value between 1 and 100, you can validate whether the input falls within this range. Similarly, if a field expects a date within a specific period, you can validate whether the input falls within that period. By enforcing range and boundary validation, you can prevent data that is outside the expected limits from being entered.

3.3.2.5 Unique Value Validation

Unique value validation ensures that the entered data is unique within a specific context. For example, if a field expects a unique username, you can validate whether the entered username already exists in the database. By enforcing unique value validation, you can prevent duplicate data from being entered, ensuring data integrity.

3.3.3 Implementing User Input Validation in C# and .NET

C# and .NET provide various mechanisms to implement user input validation. Let's explore some of the commonly used techniques:

3.3.3.1 Server-Side Validation

Server-side validation is performed on the server before processing the user input. It is the most reliable form of validation as it cannot be bypassed by the client. In C# and .NET, you can implement server-side validation using various techniques such as conditional statements, regular expressions, and custom validation methods. By validating user input on the server-side, you can ensure that only valid data is processed and stored.

3.3.3.2 Client-Side Validation

Client-side validation is performed on the client-side, typically using JavaScript, before sending the data to the server. It provides immediate feedback to users without requiring a round-trip to the server. In C# and .NET, you can implement client-side validation using frameworks like jQuery Validation or HTML5 form validation attributes. Client-side validation is useful for providing a better user experience by catching errors before submitting the form.

3.3.3.3 Combination of Server-Side and Client-Side Validation

To ensure maximum data integrity and user experience, it is often recommended to implement a combination of server-side and client-side validation. By performing validation on both the server and the client, you can provide immediate feedback to users while also ensuring that only valid data is processed and stored. This approach provides a robust validation mechanism that covers all scenarios.

3.3.4 Displaying Validation Errors

When validating user input, it is essential to provide clear and meaningful error messages to users. These error messages should explain why the input is invalid and provide guidance on how to correct it. In C# and .NET, you can display validation errors by associating error messages with the corresponding input fields. This can be achieved by using validation controls, custom error messages, or by dynamically updating the UI to highlight the incorrect fields.

3.3.5 Handling Validation Errors

When a validation error occurs, it is crucial to handle it gracefully. In C# and .NET, you can handle validation errors by displaying error messages, highlighting the incorrect fields, and preventing further processing until the errors are resolved. Additionally, you can provide options for users to correct the errors and resubmit the form. By handling validation errors effectively, you can guide users towards providing valid input and improve the overall user experience.

In this section, we explored the importance of validating user input in business applications. We discussed various types of user input validation techniques and how to implement them in C# and .NET. Additionally, we explored the importance of displaying clear error messages and handling validation errors gracefully. By implementing robust user input validation, you can enhance data integrity, improve the user experience, and prevent security vulnerabilities in your business applications.

3.4 Handling Exceptions and Errors

In any software application, errors and exceptions are inevitable. As a developer, it is crucial to handle these errors effectively to ensure the stability and reliability of your business application. In this section, we will explore various techniques and best practices for handling exceptions and errors in C# and .NET.

3.4.1 Understanding Exceptions

Exceptions are unexpected events or conditions that occur during the execution of a program, which disrupt the normal flow of the application. These can be caused by various factors such as invalid input, resource unavailability, or programming errors. When an exception occurs, it is important to catch and handle it appropriately to prevent the application from crashing or producing incorrect results.

3.4.2 Exception Handling Basics

Exception handling in C# and .NET is achieved through the use of try-catch blocks. The try block contains the code that might throw an exception, while the catch block is responsible for catching and handling the exception. Here is a basic example:

```
try
{
// Code that might throw an exception
}
catch (Exception ex)
{
// Handle the exception
}
```

In the catch block, you can perform actions such as logging the exception, displaying an error message to the user, or taking corrective measures to recover from the error. It is important to catch specific exceptions whenever possible to handle them differently based on their type.

3.4.3 Catching Specific Exceptions

C# provides a wide range of exception types that you can catch and handle individually. By catching specific exceptions, you can tailor your error handling logic to the specific error scenario. Some commonly used exception types include:

- ArgumentException: Thrown when an argument passed to a method is invalid.
- InvalidOperationException: Thrown when the state of an object is not valid for the operation being performed.
- FileNotFoundException: Thrown when a file specified in the code is not found.
- SqlException: Thrown when an error occurs while working with a SQL Server database.

To catch specific exceptions, you can use multiple catch blocks, each targeting a specific exception type. The catch blocks are evaluated in order, and the first catch block that matches the exception type is executed. Here is an example:

```
try
{
// Code that might throw an exception
}
catch (ArgumentException ex)
{
// Handle ArgumentException
}
```

```
catch (InvalidOperationException ex)
{
// Handle InvalidOperationException
}
catch (Exception ex)
{
// Handle any other exception
}
```

By catching specific exceptions, you can provide more meaningful error messages to the user and take appropriate actions to recover from the error.

3.4.4 Rethrowing Exceptions

In some cases, you may want to catch an exception, perform some additional processing, and then rethrow the exception to be handled by an outer catch block. This can be useful when you need to add additional context or information to the exception before propagating it further. To rethrow an exception, you can use the throw statement without any arguments. Here is an example:

```
try
{
// Code that might throw an exception
}
catch (Exception ex)
{
// Perform additional processing
// ...
// Rethrow the exception
throw;
}
```

By rethrowing the exception, you allow it to be caught and handled by an outer catch block, providing a centralized location for error handling and recovery.

3.4.5 Finally Block

In addition to the try and catch blocks, C# also provides a finally block that allows you to specify code that should always be executed, regardless of whether an exception occurs or not. The finally block is commonly used for cleanup tasks such as closing open resources or releasing locks. Here is an example:

```
try
{
// Code that might throw an exception
}
catch (Exception ex)
{
// Handle the exception
}
finally
{
// Cleanup tasks
}
```

The code in the finally block will be executed regardless of whether an exception occurs or not. This ensures that critical cleanup tasks are always performed, even in the presence of exceptions.

3.4.6 Logging and Error Reporting

In addition to handling exceptions, it is important to log and report errors effectively. Logging allows you to capture information about exceptions and errors, which can be useful for troubleshooting and debugging purposes. There are various logging frameworks available in

C# and .NET, such as log4net and NLog, that provide flexible and configurable logging capabilities.

When reporting errors to the user, it is important to provide clear and concise error messages that help the user understand the problem and take appropriate actions. Avoid exposing sensitive information in error messages and consider localizing error messages for internationalization purposes.

3.4.7 Best Practices for Exception Handling

To ensure effective exception handling in your business application, consider the following best practices:

- Catch specific exceptions whenever possible to handle them differently based on their type.
- Log exceptions and errors to capture valuable information for troubleshooting and debugging.
- Provide meaningful error messages to the user that help them understand the problem and take appropriate actions.
- Use the finally block to perform critical cleanup tasks, such as closing open resources.
- Avoid catching and swallowing exceptions without taking any action, as this can lead to hidden bugs and unexpected behavior.
- Consider implementing a global exception handler to catch unhandled exceptions and provide a centralized location for error handling and recovery.

By following these best practices, you can ensure that your business application handles exceptions and errors effectively, providing a robust and reliable user experience.

Conclusion

Handling exceptions and errors is a critical aspect of building business applications in C# and .NET. By understanding the basics of exception handling, catching specific exceptions, and following best practices, you can ensure that your application remains stable and reliable even in the face of unexpected events. Logging and error reporting play a crucial role in troubleshooting and debugging, while the finally block allows for proper cleanup of resources. By implementing these techniques, you can build robust and resilient business applications that provide a seamless user experience.

4 - Generating Reports in Business Apps

4.1 Introduction to Reporting in Business Apps

Reporting is an essential aspect of any business application. It allows users to analyze and visualize data, make informed decisions, and communicate information effectively. In this section, we will explore the importance of reporting in business apps and discuss various techniques and tools for generating reports.

4.1.1 The Importance of Reporting in Business Apps

Reporting plays a crucial role in business apps as it enables users to gain insights from data and make data-driven decisions. Here are some key reasons why reporting is essential in business applications:

1. **Data Analysis and Visualization**: Reports provide a way to analyze and visualize data, allowing users to identify trends, patterns, and outliers. By presenting data in a structured and meaningful manner, reports help users understand complex information quickly.

2. **Decision Making**: Reports provide valuable information that aids in decision-making processes. Whether it's sales reports, financial statements, or performance metrics, having access to accurate and up-to-date data empowers users to make informed decisions that drive business growth.

3. **Communication and Collaboration**: Reports serve as a means of communication and collaboration within an organization. They allow users to share information, present findings, and discuss strategies based on the data presented in the reports. This promotes transparency and alignment across teams and departments.

4. **Compliance and Regulatory Requirements**: Many

industries have specific compliance and regulatory requirements that necessitate accurate and auditable reporting. Business apps need to generate reports that meet these requirements, ensuring legal and regulatory compliance.

4.1.2 Reporting Techniques and Tools

There are various techniques and tools available for generating reports in business apps. Let's explore some of the commonly used ones:

1. **RDLC (Report Definition Language Client-Side)**: RDLC is a report design format used by Microsoft's reporting technology. It allows developers to create reports using Visual Studio's Report Designer, which provides a drag-and-drop interface for designing report layouts. RDLC reports can be rendered in various formats, such as PDF, Excel, or HTML, and can be embedded within Windows Forms or ASP.NET applications.

2. **Third-Party Reporting Libraries**: In addition to RDLC, there are several third-party reporting libraries available that offer advanced reporting capabilities. These libraries provide features like interactive reports, data visualization, and support for multiple data sources. Some popular third-party reporting libraries for .NET include Crystal Reports, Telerik Reporting, and DevExpress Reporting.

3. **Data Visualization Tools**: Data visualization tools, such as Power BI or Tableau, can be integrated with business apps to create interactive and visually appealing reports. These tools offer advanced data exploration and visualization capabilities, allowing users to interact with the data and gain deeper insights.

4. **Custom Reporting Solutions**: In some cases, business apps may require custom reporting solutions tailored to specific

requirements. This could involve building custom report generation logic using C# and .NET libraries or leveraging other technologies like SQL Server Reporting Services (SSRS) for enterprise-level reporting.

4.1.3 Considerations for Report Design and Generation

When designing and generating reports in business apps, there are several considerations to keep in mind:

1. **Data Source and Query Optimization**: Efficient report generation relies on optimized data retrieval and query performance. It is crucial to design and optimize the underlying data models and database queries to ensure fast and accurate report generation.

2. **Report Layout and Visualization**: The layout and visualization of reports should be intuitive and user-friendly. Consider the target audience and their specific requirements when designing the report layout. Use appropriate charts, graphs, and tables to present data in a visually appealing and understandable manner.

3. **Report Parameters and Filters**: Reports often require parameters and filters to allow users to customize the data they want to see. Implementing parameterized reports enables users to specify criteria such as date ranges, product categories, or regions, making the reports more flexible and relevant to their needs.

4. **Exporting and Printing Options**: Provide options for exporting reports to different formats like PDF, Excel, or Word. This allows users to save or share reports in their preferred format. Additionally, consider providing printing capabilities for users who prefer physical copies of reports.

5. **Report Security and Access Control**: Ensure that reports are accessible only to authorized users. Implement appropriate security measures to control access to sensitive data and restrict report generation based on user roles and permissions.

In the next section, we will delve into using RDLC for report design and generation, exploring its features and capabilities in detail.

Conclusion

Reporting is a critical component of business applications, enabling users to analyze data, make informed decisions, and communicate information effectively. In this section, we discussed the importance of reporting in business apps and explored various techniques and tools for generating reports. We also highlighted key considerations for report design and generation, emphasizing the need for optimized data sources, intuitive layouts, and secure access control. In the next section, we will dive into using RDLC for report design and generation, providing a step-by-step guide to creating reports using this technology.

4.2 Using RDLC for Report Design and Generation

In any business application, generating reports is a crucial requirement for providing valuable insights and presenting data in a structured manner. Reports help users analyze data, make informed decisions, and communicate information effectively. In this section, we will explore the usage of RDLC (Report Definition Language Client) for report design and generation in C# and .NET applications.

4.2.1 Introduction to RDLC

RDLC is a report definition language used by Microsoft's reporting technology to design and generate reports. It is a client-side reporting technology that allows you to create reports within your application without the need for a separate reporting server. RDLC reports can be rendered in various formats such as PDF, Excel, Word, and HTML.

RDLC reports are created using the Visual Studio Report Designer, which provides a drag-and-drop interface for designing the report layout. The Report Designer allows you to add data sources, define report parameters, and design the report layout by adding tables, charts, images, and other visual elements.

4.2.2 Creating RDLC Reports

To create an RDLC report, you need to follow these steps:

1. Open Visual Studio and create a new project or open an existing project.
2. Right-click on the project in the Solution Explorer and select "Add" -> "New Item".
3. In the "Add New Item" dialog, select "Reporting" under "Visual C#" and choose "Report" from the templates.

4. Give the report a meaningful name and click "Add".

5. The Report Designer will open, displaying a blank canvas where you can design the report layout.

6. To add data to the report, right-click on the "Data Sources" node in the Report Data window and select "Add New Data Source".

7. Follow the wizard to connect to your data source and select the required tables or views.

8. Once the data source is added, you can drag and drop fields from the data source onto the report layout to display the data.

9. Customize the report layout by adding tables, charts, images, and other visual elements as per your requirements.

10. Configure report parameters if needed, allowing users to filter and customize the report data.

11. Preview the report by right-clicking on the report file in the Solution Explorer and selecting "Preview".

4.2.3 Binding Data to RDLC Reports

RDLC reports can be bound to various data sources, including SQL Server databases, object collections, XML files, and web services. To bind data to an RDLC report, you need to follow these steps:

1. Open the RDLC report in the Report Designer.

2. Right-click on the report canvas and select "Report Data" to open the Report Data window.

3. In the Report Data window, right-click on "Data Sources" and select "Add New Data Source".

4. Follow the wizard to connect to your data source and select the required tables or views.

5. Once the data source is added, you can drag and drop fields from the data source onto the report layout to display the data.

6. To bind the report to a data source programmatically, you can

use the ReportViewer control in your application and set the data source programmatically using the ReportDataSource class.

4.2.4 Formatting and Customizing RDLC Reports

RDLC reports provide various formatting and customization options to enhance the visual appearance of the reports. Some of the common formatting options include:

- Changing font styles, sizes, and colors.
- Applying conditional formatting to highlight specific data based on certain conditions.
- Adding headers, footers, and page numbers.
- Grouping and sorting data.
- Adding subreports to display related data.
- Adding charts, graphs, and images to visualize data.
- Customizing report parameters and allowing users to interact with the report.

The Report Designer provides a user-friendly interface to apply these formatting options. You can select report elements, such as text boxes or tables, and use the properties window to modify their appearance and behavior.

4.2.5 Generating RDLC Reports in C# and .NET

Once you have designed the RDLC report, you can generate and display it in your C# and .NET application using the ReportViewer control. The ReportViewer control is a powerful tool that allows you to render and display RDLC reports within your application.

To generate an RDLC report in your C# and .NET application, you need to follow these steps:

1. Add a ReportViewer control to your Windows Forms or

ASP.NET application.

2. Set the ReportViewer control's processing mode to "Local" and specify the path to the RDLC report file.

3. Set the data source for the report using the ReportDataSource class.

4. Optionally, set report parameters if required.

5. Call the RefreshReport method of the ReportViewer control to generate and display the report.

The ReportViewer control takes care of rendering the report and providing navigation and printing options to the users. You can also export the report to various formats such as PDF, Excel, Word, and HTML using the built-in export functionality of the ReportViewer control.

Conclusion

RDLC reports provide a powerful and flexible solution for designing and generating reports in C# and .NET applications. With the Visual Studio Report Designer and the ReportViewer control, you can create professional-looking reports that meet the specific requirements of your business application. By following the step-by-step guide provided in this section, you will be able to leverage the capabilities of RDLC reports to enhance the reporting capabilities of your application.

4.3 Integrating Third-Party Reporting Libraries

In the previous section, we explored the use of RDLC (Report Definition Language Client) for designing and generating reports in business applications. RDLC provides a powerful and flexible way to create reports within the .NET framework. However, there may be cases where you need more advanced features or specific functionalities that are not available in RDLC. In such scenarios, integrating third-party reporting libraries can be a viable solution.

Integrating third-party reporting libraries allows you to leverage additional features and capabilities that may not be available out-of-the-box with RDLC. These libraries often provide a wide range of options for report design, data visualization, and customization. They can also offer enhanced performance and scalability, as well as support for various data sources and formats.

4.3.1 Evaluating Third-Party Reporting Libraries

Before integrating a third-party reporting library into your business application, it is essential to evaluate and choose the right library that meets your specific requirements. Here are some factors to consider during the evaluation process:

Functionality and Features

Assess the functionality and features offered by the reporting library. Consider whether it provides the necessary tools for report design, data visualization, and customization. Look for features such as interactive reports, drill-down capabilities, charting options, and support for different data sources.

Integration with .NET Framework

Ensure that the reporting library seamlessly integrates with the .NET framework and can be easily incorporated into your existing application. Check if it supports the programming language (C#) and version of the .NET framework you are using.

Performance and Scalability

Evaluate the performance and scalability of the reporting library. Consider factors such as report generation speed, handling large datasets, and support for caching and data compression. Look for libraries that offer optimizations for improved performance.

Documentation and Support

Check the availability and quality of documentation and support provided by the reporting library. Look for comprehensive documentation, tutorials, and sample code that can help you understand and utilize the library effectively. Additionally, consider the availability of technical support and community forums for troubleshooting and assistance.

Licensing and Cost

Consider the licensing model and cost associated with the reporting library. Some libraries may be open-source or have free versions available, while others may require a commercial license or subscription. Evaluate the licensing terms and ensure they align with your project's budget and requirements.

4.3.2 Integrating a Third-Party Reporting Library

Once you have selected a suitable third-party reporting library, the next step is to integrate it into your business application. The integration process may vary depending on the specific library and its requirements. However, the following steps provide a general guideline for integrating a third-party reporting library:

Step 1: Install the Reporting Library

Begin by downloading and installing the reporting library. Most libraries provide installation packages or NuGet packages that can be easily added to your project. Follow the library's documentation or installation guide for detailed instructions.

Step 2: Configure the Library

After installing the library, you may need to configure it to work with your application. This may involve setting up connection strings, configuring data sources, or specifying report templates. Refer to the library's documentation for guidance on the configuration process.

Step 3: Design Reports

Once the library is configured, you can start designing reports using the library's design tools or APIs. These tools typically provide a visual interface for designing report layouts, adding data fields, and customizing report elements. Use the library's documentation and tutorials to learn how to design reports effectively.

Step 4: Retrieve and Bind Data

To populate the reports with data, you will need to retrieve the necessary data from your application's data sources. This may involve querying databases, calling APIs, or accessing other data repositories. Once you have the data, bind it to the report's data sources using the library's APIs or data binding mechanisms.

Step 5: Generate and Display Reports

With the data bound to the report, you can generate and display the reports in your application. Depending on the library, this may involve calling specific methods or APIs to generate the reports programmatically or using built-in viewer controls to display the reports to the users.

Step 6: Customize and Enhance Reports

One of the advantages of using third-party reporting libraries is the ability to customize and enhance reports beyond the capabilities of RDLC. Explore the library's features and APIs to add interactivity, drill-down functionality, charts, graphs, and other visual elements to your reports. Use the library's documentation and examples to learn how to leverage these features effectively.

4.3.3 Considerations and Best Practices

When integrating third-party reporting libraries into your business application, keep the following considerations and best practices in mind:

Compatibility and Upgrades

Ensure that the reporting library is compatible with the version of the .NET framework and other dependencies used in your application. Stay updated with new releases and upgrades of the library to take advantage of bug fixes, performance improvements, and new features.

Performance Optimization

Optimize the performance of your reports by following best practices recommended by the reporting library. This may include techniques such as data caching, report parameterization, and efficient data retrieval. Monitor and analyze the performance of your reports to identify and address any bottlenecks.

Security and Data Protection

Take appropriate measures to secure the reports generated by the third-party library. Implement access controls, encryption, and other security measures to protect sensitive data. Ensure that the library adheres to industry-standard security practices and guidelines.

Documentation and Training

Thoroughly understand the documentation and resources provided by the reporting library. Invest time in learning the library's features, APIs, and best practices. Consider providing training to your development team to ensure they can effectively utilize the library's capabilities.

Maintenance and Support

Regularly update the reporting library to the latest version to benefit from bug fixes, performance improvements, and new features. Stay connected with the library's support channels, such as forums or technical support, to address any issues or queries that may arise during development or production.

By integrating third-party reporting libraries into your business application, you can extend the capabilities of your reporting system and provide enhanced data visualization and analysis to your users. Evaluate and choose the right library, follow the integration steps, and consider the best practices to ensure a successful implementation.

4.4 Customizing and Exporting Reports

In the previous sections, we discussed the importance of generating reports in business applications and explored different techniques for designing and generating reports using RDLC and third-party reporting libraries. In this section, we will delve deeper into customizing and exporting reports to meet the specific requirements of your business.

4.4.1 Customizing Report Layout

When it comes to customizing report layouts, it is essential to understand the specific needs and preferences of your users. Customization allows you to tailor the report's appearance and structure to provide a more intuitive and user-friendly experience. Here are some techniques you can use to customize your reports:

1. **Adding and arranging report elements**: You can add various elements to your report, such as text boxes, images, tables, and charts, to present the data in a visually appealing manner. Arrange these elements to create a logical flow and emphasize the most critical information.
2. **Formatting and styling**: Use formatting options to enhance the readability of your reports. You can apply different font styles, sizes, and colors to make the text more prominent. Additionally, you can use borders, shading, and background colors to highlight specific sections or data points.
3. **Grouping and sorting**: Grouping and sorting data in your reports can provide a more organized view of the information. You can group data based on specific criteria, such as categories or dates, and sort them in ascending or descending order. This helps users quickly identify patterns and trends in the data.

4. **Adding calculations and summaries**: Including calculations and summaries in your reports can provide users with valuable insights. You can add calculated fields to perform mathematical operations on the data, such as summing up values or calculating averages. Summaries can be displayed in the form of totals, subtotals, or grand totals.

5. **Conditional formatting**: Conditional formatting allows you to dynamically change the appearance of report elements based on specific conditions. For example, you can highlight values that meet certain criteria or apply different formatting styles based on the data's characteristics. This helps draw attention to important information or outliers.

4.4.2 Exporting Reports

In addition to customizing the report layout, it is crucial to provide users with the flexibility to export reports in various formats. Different stakeholders may have different preferences for consuming and sharing information. Here are some common export options you can offer:

1. **PDF**: Exporting reports to PDF format ensures that the document's layout and formatting remain consistent across different devices and platforms. PDF files are widely accepted and can be easily shared via email or stored for future reference.

2. **Excel**: Exporting reports to Excel format allows users to perform further analysis or manipulate the data as needed. Excel provides powerful data manipulation capabilities, such as filtering, sorting, and creating pivot tables, which can be beneficial for users who want to dive deeper into the data.

3. **Word**: Exporting reports to Word format is useful when users need to incorporate the report's content into other documents or create customized summaries. Word provides advanced

formatting options and allows users to add additional text, images, or annotations to the report.

4. **CSV**: Exporting reports to CSV (Comma-Separated Values) format is beneficial when users want to import the data into other systems or perform data migrations. CSV files are simple and can be easily opened in spreadsheet applications or imported into databases.

5. **HTML**: Exporting reports to HTML format enables users to view the report in a web browser or embed it within a web page. HTML reports can be interactive, allowing users to navigate through different sections or drill down into specific data points.

6. **Image formats**: Exporting reports to image formats, such as JPEG or PNG, can be useful when users need to include the report's visual elements in presentations or documents. Images can be easily inserted into other applications or resized without losing quality.

To provide these export options, you can leverage the built-in capabilities of reporting libraries or implement custom export functionality using the available APIs. Ensure that the exported reports maintain the same level of quality and accuracy as the original report.

4.4.3 Providing User-Friendly Report Options

In addition to customizing and exporting reports, it is essential to provide users with user-friendly options for generating and accessing reports. Here are some techniques to enhance the user experience:

1. **Report parameters**: Allow users to specify parameters such as date ranges, filters, or sorting options to customize the report's content. This empowers users to generate reports that are relevant to their specific needs.

2. **Report scheduling**: Implement a scheduling feature that

allows users to schedule reports to be generated and delivered automatically at specific intervals. This can be particularly useful for recurring reports or reports that need to be shared with multiple stakeholders.

3. **Interactive reports**: Create interactive reports that enable users to drill down into specific data points or apply filters dynamically. This allows users to explore the data in more detail and gain deeper insights.

4. **Report caching**: Implement report caching to improve performance and reduce the load on the server. Caching allows users to access previously generated reports quickly, especially when the underlying data has not changed.

By providing these user-friendly options, you can enhance the overall usability and effectiveness of your reports, ensuring that users can access the information they need in a timely and efficient manner.

Conclusion

Customizing and exporting reports are crucial aspects of building business applications. By tailoring the report layout to meet specific requirements and offering various export options, you can provide users with the flexibility and functionality they need to analyze and share information effectively. Additionally, providing user-friendly report options enhances the overall user experience and empowers users to generate and access reports that are relevant to their needs. In the next chapter, we will explore the process of deploying web-based apps to IIS, enabling users to access your application over the internet.

5 - Deploying Web-Based Apps to IIS

5.1 Understanding Web-Based Applications

In today's digital age, web-based applications have become an integral part of businesses across various industries. These applications provide a platform for organizations to deliver their services and products to a wider audience, enabling them to reach customers globally. Understanding the fundamentals of web-based applications is crucial for developers who aim to build robust and scalable enterprise applications.

5.1.1 What are Web-Based Applications?

Web-based applications, also known as web apps, are software applications that are accessed through a web browser over the internet. Unlike traditional desktop applications, web apps do not require installation on individual devices and can be accessed from any device with an internet connection. They are typically built using web technologies such as HTML, CSS, and JavaScript, and are hosted on web servers.

Web apps offer several advantages over desktop applications. They are platform-independent, meaning they can be accessed from any device or operating system. They also provide a centralized and easily updatable platform, as updates can be deployed on the server-side without requiring users to manually update their applications. Additionally, web apps can be easily scaled to accommodate a growing user base, making them ideal for enterprise-level applications.

5.1.2 Key Components of Web-Based Applications

To understand web-based applications, it is essential to familiarize yourself with their key components. These components work together to deliver a seamless user experience and ensure the functionality of the application.

1. Client-Side Technologies

The client-side of a web app refers to the part that runs on the user's device, typically a web browser. Client-side technologies include HTML, CSS, and JavaScript. HTML (Hypertext Markup Language) is used to structure the content of the web page, while CSS (Cascading Style Sheets) is used to define the visual appearance and layout. JavaScript is a programming language that adds interactivity and dynamic functionality to the web app.

2. Server-Side Technologies

The server-side of a web app refers to the part that runs on the web server. It handles the processing of requests, interacts with databases, and generates dynamic content to be sent back to the client-side. Server-side technologies include programming languages like C# and frameworks like ASP.NET. These technologies enable developers to build the business logic and handle data operations required by the web app.

3. Databases

Web apps often require persistent storage to store and retrieve data. Databases are used to store and manage the application's data. Commonly used databases in web app development include SQL Server, MySQL, and PostgreSQL. These databases allow developers to store and retrieve data efficiently, ensuring the integrity and security of the application's data.

4. Web Servers

Web servers are responsible for hosting and serving web applications to users. They receive requests from clients, process them, and send back the appropriate responses. Popular web servers include Internet Information Services (IIS) and Apache HTTP Server. Web servers also handle security, authentication, and other server-side operations required by the web app.

5.1.3 Benefits of Web-Based Applications

Web-based applications offer numerous benefits for businesses and developers alike. Understanding these benefits can help you make informed decisions when building enterprise applications.

1. Cross-Platform Compatibility

Web apps can be accessed from any device with a web browser, regardless of the operating system. This cross-platform compatibility eliminates the need to develop separate applications for different platforms, reducing development time and costs.

2. Easy Deployment and Updates

Web apps can be deployed on a central server, making it easier to manage and update the application. Updates can be rolled out seamlessly, ensuring that all users have access to the latest version of the application without requiring manual updates on individual devices.

3. Scalability and Accessibility

Web apps can handle a large number of concurrent users, making them highly scalable. They can be accessed from anywhere with an internet connection, allowing users to access the application on various devices, including desktops, laptops, tablets, and smartphones.

4. Cost-Effectiveness

Developing web-based applications can be more cost-effective compared to building native desktop applications. With web apps, there is no need to develop separate versions for different platforms, reducing development and maintenance costs.

5. Integration and Collaboration

Web apps can easily integrate with other systems and services, enabling seamless data exchange and collaboration. They can consume web APIs to interact with external services, allowing businesses to leverage existing technologies and services.

Conclusion

Understanding web-based applications is essential for developers looking to build robust and scalable enterprise applications. By grasping the key components and benefits of web apps, developers can leverage web technologies to create powerful applications that meet the needs of modern businesses. In the next section, we will explore the process of configuring IIS for hosting web apps.

5.2 Configuring IIS for Hosting Web Apps

Once you have developed a web-based application using C# and .NET, the next step is to deploy it to a web server so that it can be accessed by users over the internet. One of the most popular web servers for hosting .NET applications is Internet Information Services (IIS). In this section, we will explore the process of configuring IIS to host your web apps.

5.2.1 Installing and Setting Up IIS

Before you can start hosting your web apps on IIS, you need to ensure that it is installed and properly set up on your server. Here are the steps to install and configure IIS:

1. Open the "Server Manager" on your Windows server.
2. Click on "Add Roles and Features" to start the installation wizard.
3. Select the appropriate server from the server pool and click "Next".
4. In the "Server Roles" section, select "Web Server (IIS)" and click "Next".
5. Review the features that will be installed and click "Next".
6. On the "Role Services" screen, select the required features for your web app (e.g., ASP.NET, HTTP Activation) and click "Next".
7. Click "Install" to begin the installation process.
8. Once the installation is complete, click "Close" to exit the wizard.

5.2.2 Creating a Website in IIS

After installing IIS, the next step is to create a website that will host your web application. Here's how you can create a website in IIS:

1. Open the "Internet Information Services (IIS) Manager" from the Start menu.
2. In the left-hand pane, expand the server node and right-click on "Sites".
3. Select "Add Website" from the context menu.
4. Enter a name for your website in the "Site name" field.
5. Specify the physical path where your web application files are located.
6. Enter the host name (e.g.,) and port number for your website.
7. Select an IP address for the website or leave it as "All Unassigned" to listen on all available IP addresses.
8. Choose an appropriate protocol (HTTP or HTTPS) for your website.
9. Optionally, configure the binding to use a specific SSL certificate for HTTPS.
10. Click "OK" to create the website.

5.2.3 Configuring Application Pools

In IIS, application pools provide a way to isolate web applications from each other, ensuring that one application does not affect the performance or stability of others. Here's how you can configure application pools for your web apps:

1. Open the "Internet Information Services (IIS) Manager".
2. In the left-hand pane, expand the server node and click on "Application Pools".
3. Right-click on "DefaultAppPool" (or any other existing application pool) and select "Add Application Pool" to create

a new one.

4. Enter a name for the application pool and choose the .NET CLR version (e.g., v4.0).

5. Configure other settings such as the managed pipeline mode and start mode as per your requirements.

6. Click "OK" to create the application pool.

7. Assign the newly created application pool to your website by selecting it in the "Application Pool" dropdown while creating or editing the website.

5.2.4 Configuring Web App Settings

In addition to configuring IIS and application pools, you may need to adjust certain settings specific to your web application. Here are some common settings you might need to configure:

1. Connection Strings: If your web app uses a database, you will need to configure the connection string in the web.config file. This includes specifying the server name, database name, credentials, and other relevant details.

2. App Settings: You can define custom application settings in the web.config file, such as API keys, email server settings, or any other configuration values required by your application.

3. Security Settings: Depending on your application's security requirements, you may need to configure authentication and authorization settings in IIS. This can include enabling Windows authentication, forms authentication, or integrating with external identity providers.

4. Error Handling: Configure custom error pages or error logging mechanisms to handle and display errors gracefully to users.

5. Performance Optimization: Adjust IIS settings such as compression, caching, and request filtering to optimize the

performance of your web application.

5.2.5 Testing and Troubleshooting

Once you have configured IIS and deployed your web app, it is essential to thoroughly test it to ensure everything is working as expected. Here are some testing and troubleshooting steps you can follow:

1. Access your web app using the configured URL in a web browser to verify that it loads correctly.
2. Test different features and functionality of your web app to ensure they work as intended.
3. Monitor the IIS logs and event viewer for any errors or warnings related to your web app.
4. Use tools like Fiddler or browser developer tools to inspect network traffic and diagnose any issues.
5. If you encounter any errors, review the error messages, check the IIS logs, and search for solutions online.

By following these steps, you can successfully configure IIS to host your web apps developed using C# and .NET. Remember to regularly monitor and maintain your web server to ensure optimal performance and security.

5.3 Publishing and Deploying Web Apps

Once you have developed a web-based application using C# and .NET, the next step is to publish and deploy it to a web server. This process involves making your application accessible to users over the internet. In this section, we will explore the steps required to publish and deploy web apps, ensuring that they are accessible and secure.

5.3.1 Preparing for Deployment

Before you can publish and deploy your web app, there are a few preparations you need to make. Here are the key steps to follow:

5.3.1.1 Configuration Settings

Ensure that your web app's configuration settings are properly configured for deployment. This includes settings such as database connection strings, API keys, and any other environment-specific configurations. It is essential to have separate configurations for development, testing, and production environments.

5.3.1.2 Application Packaging

Package your web app into a deployable format. This typically involves creating a deployment package that includes all the necessary files and dependencies required to run your application. You can use tools like MSBuild or Visual Studio's Publish feature to create the deployment package.

5.3.1.3 Testing and Quality Assurance

Before deploying your web app, it is crucial to thoroughly test it to ensure that it functions as expected. Perform both functional and non-functional testing, including unit tests, integration tests, and performance tests. Additionally, conduct quality assurance checks to identify and fix any bugs or issues.

5.3.2 Publishing Web Apps

Publishing a web app involves transferring the application files to a web server and configuring the server to host the application. Here are the steps to publish your web app:

5.3.2.1 Selecting a Web Server

Choose a web server to host your application. The most common web server for hosting .NET applications is Internet Information Services (IIS). Ensure that the selected web server supports the version of .NET framework your application is built on.

5.3.2.2 Configuring the Web Server

Configure the web server to host your web app. This includes setting up the necessary application pools, virtual directories, and security settings. Ensure that the web server is properly configured to handle the expected traffic and load.

5.3.2.3 Publishing the Web App

Use the deployment package created earlier to publish your web app to the selected web server. This can be done using various methods, such as FTP, Web Deploy, or directly from Visual Studio. Follow the specific instructions provided by your web server or hosting provider to publish the application.

5.3.2.4 Verifying the Deployment

After publishing the web app, verify that it is successfully deployed and accessible. Test the application by accessing it through a web browser and performing various actions to ensure that all functionalities are working as expected. Monitor the application for any errors or issues and address them promptly.

5.3.3 Deploying Web Apps

Deploying a web app involves making it available to users and ensuring its stability and security. Here are some best practices to follow when deploying web apps:

5.3.3.1 Load Balancing and Scalability

If your web app is expected to handle a significant amount of traffic, consider implementing load balancing techniques. Load balancing distributes incoming requests across multiple servers, improving performance and ensuring high availability. Additionally, design your application to be scalable, allowing it to handle increased traffic by adding more servers or resources.

5.3.3.2 Monitoring and Logging

Implement monitoring and logging mechanisms to track the performance and health of your web app. Use tools like Application Insights or ELK stack to monitor key metrics such as response times, error rates, and resource utilization. Logging should capture relevant information for troubleshooting and auditing purposes.

5.3.3.3 Security Considerations

Ensure that your web app is secure by implementing appropriate security measures. This includes using HTTPS for secure communication, protecting against common web vulnerabilities such as cross-site scripting (XSS) and SQL injection, and implementing authentication and authorization mechanisms to control access to sensitive resources.

5.3.3.4 Continuous Deployment

Consider implementing a continuous deployment process to automate the deployment of your web app. This involves setting up a CI/CD pipeline that automatically builds, tests, and deploys your application whenever changes are made to the codebase. Tools like Azure DevOps or Jenkins can help streamline this process.

Conclusion

Publishing and deploying web apps is a critical step in making your application accessible to users. By following the steps outlined in this section, you can ensure a smooth deployment process and provide a secure and reliable experience for your users. Remember to regularly update and maintain your deployed web app to address any security vulnerabilities or performance issues that may arise.

5.4 Managing Web App Settings and Security

In this section, we will explore the important aspects of managing web app settings and security in your business applications built using C# and .NET. As your application grows and evolves, it becomes crucial to have a robust system in place to manage various settings and ensure the security of your web app.

5.4.1 Configuration Management

Configuration management plays a vital role in managing the settings and parameters of your web application. It allows you to control the behavior of your application without modifying the code. In C# and .NET, you can leverage the built-in configuration management system provided by the framework.

Configuration Files

The configuration settings for your web app are stored in configuration files. The most commonly used configuration file in a web application is the web.config file. This file contains various sections and elements that define the behavior of your application.

You can use the appSettings section to store key-value pairs of configuration settings. These settings can be accessed in your code using the ConfigurationManager.AppSettings class. This allows you to easily modify the behavior of your application without recompiling the code.

string settingValue = ConfigurationManager.AppSettings["SettingKey"];

Additionally, you can create custom configuration sections to organize your settings in a more structured manner. This can be useful when you have a large number of settings or when you want to group related settings together.

Environment-Specific Configuration

In a real-world scenario, you may have different configuration settings for different environments such as development, staging, and production. To handle this, you can create separate configuration files for each environment and use the appropriate file based on the current environment.

For example, you can have web.config for development, web.staging.config for staging, and web.production.config for production. The appropriate configuration file is automatically selected based on the environment.

This allows you to have different settings for each environment, such as database connection strings, API endpoints, and logging levels. It ensures that your application behaves correctly in each environment without the need for manual configuration changes.

5.4.2 Application Security

Security is a critical aspect of any web application. In this section, we will discuss some best practices for securing your business apps built using C# and .NET.

Authentication and Authorization

Authentication is the process of verifying the identity of a user, while authorization determines what actions a user is allowed to perform. Implementing a robust authentication and authorization system is essential to protect sensitive data and ensure that only authorized users can access certain features or resources.

In C# and .NET, you can leverage the built-in authentication and authorization mechanisms provided by the framework. The ASP.NET Identity system allows you to easily implement user authentication and manage user roles and permissions.

You can use the Authorize attribute to restrict access to certain controllers or actions based on the user's role or other criteria. For example, you can decorate a controller with [Authorize(Roles = "Admin")] to ensure that only users with the "Admin" role can access it.

```
[Authorize(Roles = "Admin")]
public class AdminController : Controller
{
// Actions for admin users
}
```

Cross-Site Scripting (XSS) Prevention

Cross-Site Scripting (XSS) is a common security vulnerability that allows attackers to inject malicious scripts into web pages viewed by other users. To prevent XSS attacks, you should always sanitize and validate user input before displaying it on your web pages.

In C# and .NET, you can use the built-in HTML encoding functions to sanitize user input. The HttpUtility.HtmlEncode method can be used to encode user input before displaying it on a web page. This ensures that any special characters are properly encoded and cannot be interpreted as HTML or JavaScript code.

```
string userInput = "<script>alert('XSS attack');</script>";
string encodedInput = HttpUtility.HtmlEncode(userInput);
```

Cross-Site Request Forgery (CSRF) Protection

Cross-Site Request Forgery (CSRF) is another common security vulnerability that allows attackers to trick users into performing unwanted actions on a website without their knowledge or consent. To protect against CSRF attacks, you should include anti-forgery tokens in your web forms.

In C# and .NET, you can use the ValidateAntiForgeryToken attribute to automatically validate anti-forgery tokens for your actions. This attribute ensures that the request is valid and originated from your web application.

```
[HttpPost]
[ValidateAntiForgeryToken]
public ActionResult SubmitForm(FormModel model)
{
// Process the form submission
}
```

5.4.3 Secure Communication

Secure communication is essential to protect sensitive data transmitted between the client and the server. In this section, we will discuss some best practices for securing communication in your web applications.

Transport Layer Security (TLS)

Transport Layer Security (TLS) is a cryptographic protocol that provides secure communication over the internet. It ensures that data transmitted between the client and the server is encrypted and cannot be intercepted or tampered with.

In C# and .NET, you can enable TLS for your web application by configuring your web server (such as IIS) to use HTTPS. This requires obtaining an SSL/TLS certificate and configuring your server to use it.

Secure Password Storage

Storing passwords securely is crucial to protect user accounts from unauthorized access. In C# and .NET, you should never store passwords in plain text. Instead, you should use a secure hashing algorithm to hash the passwords before storing them in the database.

The .NET framework provides the System.Security.Cryptography namespace, which includes various classes for secure password hashing. You can use the Rfc2898DeriveBytes class to generate a secure hash of the password.

```
string password = "myPassword";
byte[] salt = GenerateSalt();
byte[] hash = HashPassword(password, salt);
// Store the salt and hash in the database
```

Conclusion

In this section, we explored the important aspects of managing web app settings and security in your business applications built using C# and .NET. We discussed configuration management, application security, and secure communication. By following these best practices, you can ensure that your web app is secure and protected from common security vulnerabilities.

6 - Securing Business Apps with Authentication/Authorization

6.1 Introduction to App Security

In today's digital landscape, security is of utmost importance for any business application. As a developer, it is crucial to understand the fundamentals of application security and implement robust measures to protect sensitive data and ensure the integrity of your business apps. This section will provide you with an introduction to app security and guide you through the process of implementing various security measures in your C# and .NET business applications.

6.1.1 Why App Security Matters

App security plays a vital role in safeguarding your business applications from unauthorized access, data breaches, and malicious attacks. By implementing effective security measures, you can protect sensitive information, maintain the trust of your users, and comply with industry regulations. Neglecting app security can lead to severe consequences, including financial loss, reputational damage, and legal liabilities.

6.1.2 Understanding the Threat Landscape

Before diving into the implementation of app security, it is essential to understand the various threats that your business application may face. Common security threats include:

1. **Authentication Attacks**: These attacks aim to gain unauthorized access to user accounts by exploiting vulnerabilities in the authentication process. Examples include brute force attacks, password guessing, and credential

stuffing.

2. **Authorization Attacks**: Authorization attacks occur when an attacker tries to access resources or perform actions that they are not authorized to do. This can include privilege escalation, bypassing access controls, or exploiting vulnerabilities in authorization mechanisms.

3. **Injection Attacks**: Injection attacks involve injecting malicious code or commands into an application's input fields to manipulate the application's behavior. Common types of injection attacks include SQL injection, cross-site scripting (XSS), and command injection.

4. **Cross-Site Request Forgery (CSRF)**: CSRF attacks trick users into performing unwanted actions on a website without their knowledge or consent. Attackers exploit the trust between a user and a website to perform actions on behalf of the user, such as changing passwords or making unauthorized transactions.

5. **Cross-Site Scripting (XSS)**: XSS attacks involve injecting malicious scripts into web pages viewed by other users. These scripts can steal sensitive information, modify page content, or redirect users to malicious websites.

6. **Data Breaches**: Data breaches occur when unauthorized individuals gain access to sensitive data, such as user credentials, personal information, or financial records. Data breaches can lead to identity theft, financial fraud, and reputational damage.

Understanding these threats will help you design and implement appropriate security measures to protect your business application.

6.1.3 Implementing User Authentication

User authentication is a fundamental aspect of app security. It ensures that only authorized users can access the application and its resources. There are various authentication mechanisms available, including:

1. **Username and Password**: The most common authentication method, where users provide a username and password to access the application. It is essential to enforce strong password policies, such as minimum length, complexity requirements, and password expiration.

2. **Multi-Factor Authentication (MFA)**: MFA adds an extra layer of security by requiring users to provide additional authentication factors, such as a one-time password (OTP) sent to their mobile device or a fingerprint scan.

3. **Social Login**: Social login allows users to authenticate using their existing social media accounts, such as Google, Facebook, or Twitter. This method simplifies the authentication process for users while leveraging the security measures implemented by the social media platforms.

4. **Single Sign-On (SSO)**: SSO enables users to authenticate once and access multiple applications without re-entering their credentials. It improves user experience and reduces the risk of password-related vulnerabilities.

When implementing user authentication, it is crucial to store user credentials securely. Avoid storing passwords in plain text and instead use strong hashing algorithms, such as bcrypt or Argon2, to store password hashes.

6.1.4 Managing User Roles and Permissions

Once users are authenticated, it is essential to manage their roles and permissions to control access to different parts of the application.

Role-based access control (RBAC) is a common approach to managing user roles and permissions. RBAC allows you to assign specific roles to users and define the permissions associated with each role.

For example, in an HR application, you may have roles such as "HR Manager," "Employee," and "Administrator." The HR Manager role may have permissions to view and edit employee records, while the Employee role may only have permission to view their own records. The Administrator role may have full access to all features and functionality.

Implementing RBAC involves defining roles, associating permissions with each role, and enforcing these permissions throughout the application. It is essential to regularly review and update roles and permissions as the application evolves and new features are added.

6.1.5 Securing Data and APIs

In addition to user authentication and authorization, it is crucial to secure data and APIs within your business application. Here are some key considerations:

1. **Data Encryption**: Encrypt sensitive data at rest and in transit to protect it from unauthorized access. Use industry-standard encryption algorithms and protocols, such as AES and SSL/TLS, to ensure the confidentiality and integrity of data.

2. **Input Validation**: Validate and sanitize all user input to prevent injection attacks, such as SQL injection and XSS. Use parameterized queries or stored procedures to mitigate the risk of SQL injection. Implement output encoding to prevent XSS attacks.

3. **API Security**: If your application exposes APIs for integration with other systems, ensure that these APIs are secure. Implement authentication and authorization

mechanisms for API access. Use secure communication protocols, such as HTTPS, to protect data transmitted through APIs.

4. **Error Handling**: Implement proper error handling and logging mechanisms to capture and handle exceptions securely. Avoid exposing sensitive information in error messages, as it can be exploited by attackers.

By implementing these security measures, you can significantly reduce the risk of security breaches and protect your business application and its data.

Conclusion

App security is a critical aspect of building business applications in C# and .NET. By understanding the threat landscape, implementing user authentication, managing user roles and permissions, and securing data and APIs, you can ensure the integrity and confidentiality of your application. In the next section, we will explore the implementation of user authentication in detail.

6.2 Implementing User Authentication

User authentication is a critical aspect of building business applications. It ensures that only authorized users can access the application and its resources. In this section, we will explore the process of implementing user authentication in your C# and .NET business app.

6.2.1 Understanding User Authentication

Before diving into the implementation details, let's first understand the concept of user authentication. User authentication is the process of verifying the identity of a user attempting to access a system or application. It ensures that the user is who they claim to be and grants them access based on their credentials.

In the context of a business application, user authentication plays a vital role in protecting sensitive data and ensuring that only authorized individuals can perform specific actions within the application. By implementing user authentication, you can enforce security measures and control access to various features and functionalities.

6.2.2 Choosing an Authentication Method

When implementing user authentication in your C# and .NET business app, you have several authentication methods to choose from. The most common methods include:

1. Forms Authentication: This method involves creating a login form where users enter their credentials (such as username and password). The application then verifies these credentials against a user database and grants access if they are valid.

2. Windows Authentication: With this method, the application relies on the user's Windows credentials to authenticate them.

It is suitable for intranet applications where users are already authenticated by their Windows domain.

3. OAuth/OpenID Connect: These authentication protocols allow users to authenticate using their existing social media or third-party accounts (such as Google or Facebook). The application relies on the authentication provider to verify the user's identity.

The choice of authentication method depends on your application's requirements, the target audience, and the level of security needed. For example, if your application is an internal business tool, Windows Authentication might be the most suitable option. On the other hand, if you want to provide a seamless login experience for users, OAuth/OpenID Connect could be a good choice.

6.2.3 Implementing Forms Authentication

In this section, we will focus on implementing forms authentication, which is one of the most commonly used authentication methods in business applications. Forms authentication allows users to log in using a username and password combination.

To implement forms authentication in your C# and .NET business app, follow these steps:

1. Create a login form: Design a user interface that prompts users to enter their credentials. This form should include input fields for the username and password.

2. Validate user credentials: When the user submits the login form, retrieve the entered credentials and validate them against a user database. You can use techniques like hashing and salting to securely store and compare passwords.

3. Generate an authentication token: If the user's credentials are valid, generate an authentication token that represents their session. This token should be unique and securely generated.

4. Store the authentication token: Store the authentication token in a secure location, such as a session variable or a cookie. This token will be used to identify the user throughout their session.

5. Grant access to authorized resources: Once the user is authenticated, grant them access to the authorized resources within your application. This can be achieved by checking the authentication token on each request and verifying the user's permissions.

6. Implement logout functionality: Provide a way for users to log out of the application. When the user logs out, invalidate their authentication token and redirect them to the login page.

By following these steps, you can successfully implement forms authentication in your C# and .NET business app. Remember to consider security best practices, such as using secure password storage techniques and protecting against common vulnerabilities like cross-site scripting (XSS) and cross-site request forgery (CSRF).

6.2.4 Enhancing User Authentication with Additional Features

While basic user authentication provides a solid foundation for securing your business app, you can enhance it further by incorporating additional features. Some of these features include:

1. Password reset functionality: Allow users to reset their passwords if they forget them. This can be achieved by sending a password reset link to the user's registered email address.

2. Account lockout: Implement a mechanism that locks user accounts after a certain number of failed login attempts. This helps prevent brute-force attacks and unauthorized access.

3. Two-factor authentication (2FA): Implement an additional layer of security by requiring users to provide a second form of

authentication, such as a verification code sent to their mobile device.

4. Role-based access control: Assign different roles to users and define access permissions based on these roles. This allows you to control which features and functionalities each user can access.

By incorporating these additional features, you can further enhance the security and usability of your C# and .NET business app.

Conclusion

Implementing user authentication is a crucial step in building secure business applications. By choosing the appropriate authentication method, such as forms authentication, and following the necessary steps, you can ensure that only authorized users can access your application and its resources. Additionally, by incorporating additional features like password reset functionality and role-based access control, you can further enhance the security and usability of your application.

6.3 Managing User Roles and Permissions

In any business application, it is crucial to have proper user role management and permission control to ensure the security and integrity of the system. Managing user roles and permissions allows you to control access to different features and functionalities based on the user's role and responsibilities within the organization. This section will guide you through the process of implementing user roles and permissions in your C# and .NET business application.

6.3.1 Understanding User Roles and Permissions

Before diving into the implementation details, it is essential to have a clear understanding of user roles and permissions. User roles define the different roles or positions within the organization, such as administrator, manager, employee, or customer. Each role has specific responsibilities and access rights within the application.

Permissions, on the other hand, define the actions or operations that a user can perform within the application. For example, an administrator might have permissions to create, read, update, and delete records, while an employee might only have permission to view and update their own records.

By defining user roles and assigning appropriate permissions, you can ensure that users can only access the features and data that are relevant to their role and responsibilities.

6.3.2 Designing User Roles and Permissions

The first step in managing user roles and permissions is to design the roles and permissions structure for your application. This involves identifying the different roles within your organization and defining the permissions associated with each role.

Start by listing all the roles that exist within your organization. For example, you might have roles like administrator, manager, employee, and customer. Next, identify the different actions or operations that each role should be able to perform. This could include creating, reading, updating, and deleting records, as well as other specific actions related to your application's functionality.

Once you have identified the roles and their associated permissions, you can create a role-based access control (RBAC) system in your application. RBAC allows you to assign roles to users and manage their permissions based on those roles.

6.3.3 Implementing Role-Based Access Control

In C# and .NET, you can implement role-based access control using various techniques and frameworks. One common approach is to use the built-in ASP.NET Identity framework, which provides a robust and flexible solution for managing user roles and permissions.

To implement role-based access control using ASP.NET Identity, follow these steps:

1. Configure ASP.NET Identity: Start by configuring ASP.NET Identity in your application. This involves setting up the necessary database tables and configuring the authentication and authorization settings.

2. Define Roles: Next, define the roles that exist within your application. You can do this by creating a new role manager and using the CreateAsync method to create roles programmatically or by manually adding roles to the database.

3. Assign Roles to Users: Once you have defined the roles, you can assign them to users. This can be done during the user registration process or by providing an interface for administrators to manage user roles.

4. Check User Roles and Permissions: In your application's code,

you can check the user's role and permissions to determine whether they have access to certain features or actions. You can use the UserManager and RoleManager classes provided by ASP.NET Identity to retrieve the user's roles and check their permissions.

5. Implement Role-Based Authorization: Finally, implement role-based authorization in your application's controllers and actions. You can use the [Authorize] attribute with role-based parameters to restrict access to specific roles. For example, [Authorize(Roles = "Administrator")] would only allow users with the "Administrator" role to access the decorated action.

By following these steps, you can effectively implement role-based access control in your C# and .NET business application.

6.3.4 Managing User Permissions

In addition to assigning roles to users, you may also need to manage user-specific permissions. User-specific permissions allow you to grant or revoke specific permissions for individual users, overriding the permissions associated with their assigned role.

To implement user-specific permissions, you can create a separate table in your database to store user permissions. This table can have a many-to-many relationship with the user table, allowing you to assign multiple permissions to each user.

In your application's code, you can then check both the user's role and their individual permissions to determine their access rights. This allows for more granular control over user permissions and can be useful in scenarios where certain users require additional or restricted access beyond their assigned role.

Conclusion

Managing user roles and permissions is a critical aspect of building secure and robust business applications. By properly designing and implementing role-based access control, you can ensure that users have the appropriate access rights based on their roles and responsibilities within the organization. Additionally, managing user-specific permissions allows for more granular control over access rights, providing flexibility in granting or revoking specific permissions for individual users.

6.4 Securing Data and APIs

Securing data and APIs is a critical aspect of building business applications. In today's interconnected world, where data breaches and unauthorized access are becoming increasingly common, it is essential to implement robust security measures to protect sensitive information and ensure the integrity of your application.

In this section, we will explore various techniques and best practices for securing data and APIs in your C# and .NET business applications. We will cover topics such as encryption, authentication, authorization, and securing communication channels. By the end of this section, you will have a solid understanding of how to implement effective security measures to safeguard your application and its data.

6.4.1 Securing Data

Data security is a fundamental aspect of any business application. Whether you are dealing with customer information, financial data, or any other sensitive information, it is crucial to protect it from unauthorized access or tampering. Here are some key considerations for securing data in your application:

6.4.1.1 Encryption

Encryption is a powerful technique that ensures data confidentiality by converting it into an unreadable format. By encrypting sensitive data, even if it falls into the wrong hands, it will be useless without the decryption key. In your C# and .NET applications, you can leverage cryptographic libraries and algorithms to implement encryption and decryption functionality. Use strong encryption algorithms such as AES (Advanced Encryption Standard) to ensure the highest level of security.

6.4.1.2 Secure Storage

Storing sensitive data securely is crucial to prevent unauthorized access. When designing your data storage architecture, consider using secure storage mechanisms such as encrypted databases or encrypted file systems. Additionally, ensure that access to the data storage is restricted to authorized personnel only, and implement strong access control measures.

6.4.1.3 Data Masking

Data masking is a technique used to protect sensitive data by replacing it with fictitious or obfuscated values. This is particularly useful when dealing with non-production environments or when sharing data with third-party vendors for testing purposes. By masking sensitive data, you can ensure that it remains protected while still allowing the application to function as intended.

6.4.2 Securing APIs

APIs (Application Programming Interfaces) play a crucial role in modern business applications, enabling integration with external systems and facilitating data exchange. However, APIs can also be a potential security vulnerability if not properly secured. Here are some best practices for securing APIs in your C# and .NET applications:

6.4.2.1 Authentication

Authentication is the process of verifying the identity of a user or system accessing an API. Implementing strong authentication mechanisms, such as username/password authentication or token-based authentication, is essential to ensure that only authorized entities can access your APIs. Consider using industry-standard protocols like OAuth or JWT (JSON Web Tokens) for secure authentication.

6.4.2.2 Authorization

Authorization determines what actions a user or system can perform once they have been authenticated. It is essential to implement fine-grained authorization mechanisms to control access to different API endpoints or resources. Role-based access control (RBAC) or attribute-based access control (ABAC) are commonly used authorization models that can be implemented in your C# and .NET applications.

6.4.2.3 Secure Communication

Securing the communication channel between your application and the API is crucial to prevent eavesdropping or tampering of data. Always use secure protocols such as HTTPS (HTTP over SSL/TLS) to encrypt the data transmitted between the client and the server. Additionally, consider implementing certificate-based authentication to ensure the authenticity of the server.

6.4.2.4 Rate Limiting and Throttling

To protect your APIs from abuse or denial-of-service attacks, it is essential to implement rate limiting and throttling mechanisms. Rate limiting restricts the number of requests a client can make within a specific time period, while throttling limits the number of requests processed by the server. These measures help ensure the availability and stability of your APIs.

6.4.3 Security Auditing and Monitoring

Implementing security measures is not a one-time task; it requires continuous monitoring and auditing to identify and address potential vulnerabilities. Here are some practices to consider:

6.4.3.1 Logging and Auditing

Implement comprehensive logging and auditing mechanisms to track and monitor user activities, API requests, and system events. Log critical information such as authentication attempts, access control failures, and any suspicious activities. Regularly review and analyze the logs to identify potential security issues and take appropriate actions.

6.4.3.2 Intrusion Detection and Prevention

Consider implementing intrusion detection and prevention systems (IDPS) to monitor network traffic and detect any unauthorized access attempts or malicious activities. IDPS can help identify potential security breaches and trigger alerts or take automated actions to mitigate the risks.

6.4.3.3 Regular Security Assessments

Perform regular security assessments and penetration testing to identify vulnerabilities in your application and infrastructure. Engage security professionals or ethical hackers to simulate real-world attacks and provide recommendations for improving the security posture of your application.

In conclusion, securing data and APIs is of utmost importance in building business applications. By implementing encryption, secure storage, authentication, authorization, and secure communication, you can protect sensitive data and ensure the integrity of your application.

Additionally, regular security auditing and monitoring help identify and address potential vulnerabilities, ensuring the ongoing security of your application.

7 - Integrating with Web APIs

7.1 Understanding Web APIs and Integration

In today's interconnected world, integrating different systems and applications is crucial for the success of any business. Web APIs (Application Programming Interfaces) play a vital role in enabling this integration by allowing different software applications to communicate and share data with each other. Understanding how to work with Web APIs is essential for building modern business applications that can seamlessly interact with other systems.

7.1.1 What are Web APIs?

A Web API is a set of rules and protocols that allows different software applications to communicate with each other over the internet. It provides a standardized way for applications to request and exchange data, perform actions, and access functionality provided by another application or service.

Web APIs are typically built using HTTP (Hypertext Transfer Protocol) and follow the principles of REST (Representational State Transfer). RESTful APIs use standard HTTP methods such as GET, POST, PUT, and DELETE to perform operations on resources exposed by the API.

7.1.2 Benefits of Web API Integration

Integrating with Web APIs offers several benefits for business applications:

1. **Data Exchange**: Web APIs enable the exchange of data between different systems, allowing applications to access and utilize information from external sources.

2. **Functionality Extension**: By integrating with Web APIs, applications can leverage the functionality and services provided by other systems, enhancing their own capabilities.

3. **Automation and Efficiency**: Web API integration enables automation of tasks and processes by allowing applications to interact with external systems programmatically, reducing manual effort and improving efficiency.

4. **Real-time Updates**: Web APIs facilitate real-time data synchronization and updates between systems, ensuring that information is always up-to-date across different applications.

5. **Ecosystem Integration**: Web API integration allows businesses to connect with third-party services, partners, and platforms, expanding their reach and enabling collaboration within a larger ecosystem.

7.1.3 Types of Web APIs

There are different types of Web APIs that serve various purposes. Some common types include:

1. **Public APIs**: These APIs are publicly available and can be accessed by any developer. They are often provided by popular platforms and services, such as social media platforms, payment gateways, and mapping services.

2. **Private APIs**: Private APIs are designed for internal use within an organization. They are used to expose functionality and data to internal applications and systems.

3. **Partner APIs**: Partner APIs are specifically designed for integration with trusted partners and third-party systems. They provide controlled access to specific functionality or data.

4. **Custom APIs**: Custom APIs are developed by organizations to expose their own services and functionality to external

applications. These APIs are tailored to meet the specific needs of the organization.

7.1.4 Integration Approaches

When integrating with Web APIs, there are different approaches that can be taken based on the requirements and capabilities of the systems involved:

1. **Direct Integration**: In this approach, the business application directly communicates with the Web API using HTTP requests and handles the data exchange and processing. This approach provides more control and flexibility but requires more development effort.

2. **API Libraries and SDKs**: Many Web APIs provide libraries or SDKs (Software Development Kits) that abstract the underlying communication and provide a higher-level interface for interacting with the API. These libraries often provide pre-built functions and classes that simplify the integration process.

3. **Integration Platforms**: Integration platforms, such as iPaaS (Integration Platform as a Service), provide a centralized hub for managing and orchestrating integrations between different systems. These platforms offer visual tools and connectors to simplify the integration process and provide features like data mapping, transformation, and workflow automation.

7.1.5 Considerations for Web API Integration

When integrating with Web APIs, there are several considerations to keep in mind:

1. **API Documentation**: Always refer to the API

documentation provided by the API provider. It contains important information about the API endpoints, request/response formats, authentication requirements, and any limitations or restrictions.

2. **Authentication and Authorization**: Most Web APIs require authentication to ensure secure access. Understand the authentication mechanisms supported by the API and implement the necessary authentication logic in your application.

3. **Error Handling**: Handle errors and exceptions that may occur during API integration gracefully. Implement appropriate error handling mechanisms to handle API failures, network issues, and invalid responses.

4. **Rate Limiting**: Some APIs impose rate limits to prevent abuse and ensure fair usage. Be aware of any rate limits imposed by the API and design your application to handle rate limit restrictions.

5. **Data Mapping and Transformation**: When integrating with different systems, data may need to be transformed or mapped between different formats or structures. Ensure that you have mechanisms in place to handle data mapping and transformation as required.

6. **Testing and Monitoring**: Thoroughly test your integration with the Web API to ensure that it functions as expected. Implement monitoring and logging mechanisms to track API usage, identify issues, and troubleshoot integration problems.

By understanding the fundamentals of Web APIs and the integration process, you will be well-equipped to build business applications that can seamlessly communicate and exchange data with other systems. In the next section, we will explore how to consume Web APIs in C# and .NET applications.

7.2 Consuming Web APIs in Business Apps

In today's interconnected world, businesses often rely on various external services and systems to enhance their applications and provide additional functionality. Web APIs (Application Programming Interfaces) play a crucial role in enabling this integration by allowing different applications to communicate and exchange data seamlessly. In this section, we will explore the process of consuming web APIs in business apps, enabling you to leverage the power of external services to enhance your application's capabilities.

7.2.1 Understanding Web API Consumption

Before diving into the details of consuming web APIs, it is essential to understand the concept and purpose of web APIs. A web API is a set of rules and protocols that allows different software applications to communicate with each other. It enables your application to interact with external services, retrieve data, and perform various operations.

When consuming a web API, your application acts as a client, making requests to the API and receiving responses in return. These requests and responses are typically in the form of HTTP (Hypertext Transfer Protocol) messages, which include headers, request methods, and data payloads.

Web APIs can provide a wide range of functionalities, such as retrieving data from a remote server, submitting data, performing calculations, or even triggering specific actions on the server-side. By consuming web APIs, you can leverage the capabilities of external services without having to build everything from scratch.

7.2.2 Choosing the Right Web API

Before integrating a web API into your business app, it is crucial to choose the right API that aligns with your application's requirements and objectives. Consider the following factors when selecting a web API:

1. **Functionality**: Ensure that the API provides the specific functionality you need. Evaluate the available endpoints, methods, and data formats to determine if they meet your application's requirements.

2. **Documentation**: Look for well-documented APIs that provide clear instructions on how to consume them. Good documentation should include details about authentication, request/response formats, error handling, and any limitations or restrictions.

3. **Reliability and Performance**: Consider the reliability and performance of the API. Look for APIs that have a good track record of uptime and responsiveness. Check if the API offers any performance metrics or guarantees.

4. **Authentication and Authorization**: Determine the authentication and authorization mechanisms supported by the API. Ensure that the API provides secure access control mechanisms to protect your application and data.

5. **Scalability**: Consider the scalability of the API. If your application is expected to handle a large volume of requests, ensure that the API can handle the expected load and scale accordingly.

6. **Support and Community**: Look for APIs that have an active support team and a vibrant community. Having access to support resources and a community of developers can be invaluable when facing challenges or seeking guidance.

By carefully evaluating these factors, you can choose a web API that best fits your application's needs and ensures a smooth integration process.

7.2.3 Consuming Web APIs in C# and .NET

Once you have selected the appropriate web API for your business app, it's time to start consuming it within your C# and .NET application. The process of consuming a web API typically involves the following steps:

1. **Identify API Endpoints**: Review the API documentation to identify the available endpoints and the corresponding HTTP methods (GET, POST, PUT, DELETE, etc.). Each endpoint represents a specific functionality or resource provided by the API.

2. **HTTP Requests**: Use the HttpClient class in C# to send HTTP requests to the API endpoints. The HttpClient class provides methods for sending GET, POST, PUT, DELETE, and other types of requests. You can specify the request headers, parameters, and payload data as required by the API.

3. **Handle Responses**: Once the API receives your request, it will process it and send back a response. Use the HttpResponseMessage class to handle the response received from the API. You can access the response status code, headers, and content.

4. **Deserialize Response**: If the API returns data in a structured format such as JSON or XML, you need to deserialize the response content into C# objects. Use libraries like Newtonsoft.Json or System.Xml.Serialization to parse and deserialize the response data into strongly-typed objects.

5. **Error Handling**: Implement error handling logic to handle any errors or exceptions that may occur during the API request/response process. Handle different HTTP status codes and error messages returned by the API and take appropriate actions in your application.

6. **Authentication and Authorization**: If the API requires

authentication or authorization, you need to include the necessary credentials or tokens in the request headers. Follow the authentication mechanisms specified by the API documentation, such as API keys, OAuth, or token-based authentication.

7. **Testing and Debugging**: During the development process, thoroughly test and debug your API integration code. Use tools like Postman or Fiddler to simulate API requests and verify the responses. Debug any issues or unexpected behavior using the debugging capabilities of Visual Studio.

By following these steps, you can successfully consume web APIs in your C# and .NET business applications, enabling seamless integration with external services and unlocking new functionalities for your users.

7.2.4 Best Practices for Consuming Web APIs

To ensure a smooth and efficient integration process, consider the following best practices when consuming web APIs in your business apps:

1. **Use Asynchronous Programming**: When making API requests, use asynchronous programming techniques like async and await to prevent blocking the main thread and improve the responsiveness of your application.

2. **Implement Caching**: If the API responses are relatively static or have a long expiration time, consider implementing caching mechanisms to reduce the number of API requests and improve performance.

3. **Handle Rate Limiting**: Some APIs impose rate limits to prevent abuse or ensure fair usage. Implement logic to handle rate limiting by respecting the API's rate limits and handling any rate limit exceeded errors gracefully.

4. **Implement Retry Logic**: Network issues or temporary server

failures can cause API requests to fail. Implement retry logic to automatically retry failed requests with exponential backoff to improve the reliability of your application.

5. **Monitor API Usage**: Monitor the usage of the APIs in your application to identify any performance issues, errors, or potential bottlenecks. Use logging and monitoring tools to track API requests, response times, and error rates.

6. **Keep API Keys and Secrets Secure**: When using APIs that require authentication or API keys, ensure that you securely store and manage these keys and secrets. Avoid hardcoding them in your code or exposing them in public repositories.

By following these best practices, you can ensure a robust and efficient integration of web APIs into your business applications, providing enhanced functionality and seamless integration with external services.

Conclusion

In this section, we explored the process of consuming web APIs in business apps. We discussed the importance of choosing the right API, the steps involved in consuming web APIs in C# and .NET, and best practices to follow during the integration process. By effectively leveraging web APIs, you can enhance your application's capabilities, integrate with external services, and provide a seamless experience for your users.

7.3 Handling API Authentication and Authorization

In today's interconnected world, integrating with web APIs has become a crucial aspect of building business applications. However, when working with APIs, it is essential to ensure that the data and functionality being accessed are secure and only accessible to authorized users. This is where API authentication and authorization come into play. In this section, we will explore the various techniques and best practices for handling API authentication and authorization in your C# and .NET business applications.

7.3.1 Understanding API Authentication

API authentication is the process of verifying the identity of the client making the API request. It ensures that only authorized users or applications can access the API's resources. There are several authentication mechanisms available, and the choice depends on the specific requirements of your application and the API you are integrating with. Let's explore some common authentication methods:

7.3.1.1 API Keys

API keys are a simple and widely used method for authenticating API requests. Each client is assigned a unique API key, which is included in the request headers or query parameters. The server validates the API key to authenticate the client. API keys are typically used for public APIs or when the authentication requirements are relatively low.

7.3.1.2 OAuth 2.0

OAuth 2.0 is an industry-standard protocol for authorization. It allows users to grant limited access to their resources on one site to another site without sharing their credentials. OAuth 2.0 involves multiple parties: the client application, the API provider, and the user. The client application obtains an access token from the API provider, which is then used to authenticate subsequent API requests. OAuth 2.0

provides a secure and scalable authentication mechanism suitable for a wide range of scenarios.

7.3.1.3 JSON Web Tokens (JWT)

JSON Web Tokens (JWT) are a compact and self-contained method for securely transmitting information between parties as a JSON object. JWTs consist of three parts: a header, a payload, and a signature. The payload contains the claims, which can include information about the user, permissions, and other relevant data. JWTs are often used for stateless authentication, where the server can verify the token's authenticity without the need for a centralized session store.

7.3.2 Implementing API Authentication in C# and .NET

Now that we have a basic understanding of API authentication methods let's explore how to implement them in C# and .NET. We will focus on OAuth 2.0 and JWT authentication methods, as they are widely used and provide robust security.

7.3.2.1 OAuth 2.0 Authentication

To implement OAuth 2.0 authentication in your C# and .NET application, you can leverage existing libraries and frameworks that provide OAuth 2.0 support. One popular library is IdentityServer, which is an open-source framework for implementing OAuth 2.0 and OpenID Connect protocols. IdentityServer simplifies the process of integrating OAuth 2.0 authentication into your application by providing a set of APIs and components.

To get started with OAuth 2.0 authentication using IdentityServer, you need to perform the following steps:

1. Set up an IdentityServer instance: Install the IdentityServer NuGet package and configure the necessary settings, such as client applications, API resources, and user stores.
2. Configure client applications: Register your client applications with IdentityServer and configure the required scopes and permissions.
3. Implement authentication endpoints: Create the necessary endpoints in your application to handle the OAuth 2.0 authentication flow, such as the authorization endpoint, token endpoint, and callback endpoint.
4. Secure API endpoints: Protect your API endpoints by validating the access tokens issued by IdentityServer. You can use middleware like UseAuthentication and UseAuthorization to enforce authentication and authorization rules.

7.3.2.2 JWT Authentication

Implementing JWT authentication in your C# and .NET application involves generating and validating JWTs. There are several libraries available that simplify the process of working with JWTs, such as System.IdentityModel.Tokens.Jwt and Microsoft.AspNetCore.Authentication.JwtBearer.

To implement JWT authentication, follow these steps:

1. Generate JWTs: When a user successfully authenticates, generate a JWT containing the necessary claims, such as user ID, roles, and permissions. Sign the JWT using a secret key or a certificate.
2. Validate JWTs: In your API endpoints, validate the incoming JWTs to ensure their authenticity and integrity. Verify the signature, validate the claims, and check if the token is not expired.

3. Secure API endpoints: Use middleware like UseAuthentication and UseAuthorization to enforce JWT authentication and authorization rules. This ensures that only requests with valid JWTs can access protected resources.

7.3.3 Handling API Authorization

API authorization determines what actions a user or client can perform once they are authenticated. It involves defining roles, permissions, and access control rules to restrict or allow access to specific resources or operations. Let's explore some common techniques for handling API authorization:

7.3.3.1 Role-Based Access Control (RBAC)

Role-Based Access Control (RBAC) is a widely used authorization model that assigns permissions to roles and then assigns roles to users. RBAC simplifies the management of permissions by grouping them into roles, making it easier to assign and revoke access rights. In your C# and .NET application, you can implement RBAC by defining roles and associating them with users or client applications. Then, you can use middleware or custom authorization filters to check if the authenticated user or client has the necessary role to access a particular resource.

7.3.3.2 Attribute-Based Access Control (ABAC)

Attribute-Based Access Control (ABAC) is a more fine-grained authorization model that considers various attributes of the user, resource, and environment to make access control decisions. ABAC uses policies defined in terms of attributes and conditions to determine whether a user or client has access to a resource. In C# and .NET, you can implement ABAC by using custom authorization filters or by leveraging frameworks like Policy-based Authorization in ASP.NET Core.

7.3.4 Best Practices for API Authentication and Authorization

To ensure the security and integrity of your API authentication and authorization mechanisms, consider the following best practices:

1. Use secure communication protocols: Always use HTTPS to encrypt the communication between your application and the API server. This prevents eavesdropping and tampering of sensitive data.

2. Implement rate limiting: Protect your API from abuse by implementing rate limiting mechanisms. This prevents brute-force attacks and ensures fair usage of your API resources.

3. Keep secrets secure: Store API keys, client secrets, and other sensitive information securely. Avoid hardcoding secrets in your source code or configuration files. Instead, use secure storage mechanisms like Azure Key Vault or environment variables.

4. Regularly rotate secrets: Periodically rotate your API keys, client secrets, and other credentials to minimize the impact of a potential security breach.

5. Implement multi-factor authentication (MFA): Consider implementing MFA for your API authentication to provide an additional layer of security. This can involve using SMS-based verification codes, email-based verification, or hardware tokens.

6. Audit and monitor API access: Implement logging and monitoring mechanisms to track API usage and detect any suspicious activities. Regularly review the logs to identify potential security issues or anomalies.

By following these best practices, you can ensure that your API authentication and authorization mechanisms are robust and secure, protecting your application and its data from unauthorized access.

Conclusion

In this section, we explored the importance of API authentication and authorization in building secure business applications. We discussed various authentication methods such as API keys, OAuth 2.0, and JSON Web Tokens (JWT), along with their implementation in C# and .NET. Additionally, we explored authorization techniques like Role-Based Access Control (RBAC) and Attribute-Based Access Control (ABAC). Finally, we highlighted some best practices to ensure the security and integrity of your API authentication and authorization mechanisms. By implementing these techniques and following best practices, you can build robust and secure business applications that integrate seamlessly with web APIs.

7.4 Working with API Responses and Error Handling

When building business applications that integrate with web APIs, it is crucial to understand how to handle API responses and errors effectively. APIs often return various types of responses, including success responses, error responses, and other informational responses. In this section, we will explore best practices for working with API responses and implementing robust error handling mechanisms in your C# and .NET applications.

7.4.1 Understanding API Responses

Before diving into handling API responses, it is essential to understand the different types of responses you may encounter when interacting with web APIs. Here are some common types of API responses:

1. Success Responses: These responses indicate that the API request was successful, and the desired data or action has been returned or performed. Success responses typically have a status code in the 2xx range, such as 200 (OK) or 201 (Created).

2. Error Responses: Error responses occur when an API request encounters an issue or fails to complete successfully. These responses usually have a status code in the 4xx or 5xx range, such as 400 (Bad Request) or 500 (Internal Server Error). Error responses often include additional information, such as error messages or error codes, to help identify the cause of the issue.

3. Informational Responses: These responses provide additional information about the API request or the server's status. Informational responses have status codes in the 1xx range, such as 100 (Continue) or 101 (Switching Protocols).

4. Redirect Responses: Redirect responses indicate that the requested resource has moved temporarily or permanently to a different location. These responses have status codes in the 3xx range, such as 301 (Moved Permanently) or 302 (Found).

Understanding these different types of API responses is crucial for effectively handling and processing the data returned by the API.

7.4.2 Handling API Responses

When working with API responses in your C# and .NET applications, it is essential to handle them appropriately to ensure a smooth user experience and proper application functionality. Here are some best practices for handling API responses:

1. Parsing and Deserializing Responses: Most APIs return data in a structured format, such as JSON or XML. To work with this data in your application, you need to parse and deserialize the API response into appropriate data structures or objects. C# provides various libraries and frameworks, such as Newtonsoft.Json, to simplify the parsing and deserialization process.

2. Validating Responses: Before using the data returned by an API, it is crucial to validate it to ensure its integrity and correctness. Validate the response against the expected data structure and perform any necessary data validation checks. This step helps prevent potential issues caused by malformed or unexpected data.

3. Handling Success Responses: When an API request is successful, you need to handle the returned data appropriately. Update your application's state, display the data to the user, or perform any necessary actions based on the success response. Ensure that your application gracefully handles different success scenarios and provides appropriate feedback to the user.

4. Handling Error Responses: Error responses require special attention to ensure that your application handles them gracefully. Depending on the type of error, you may need to display error messages to the user, log the error for debugging purposes, or take corrective actions. Implement a consistent error handling mechanism that provides meaningful error messages and helps users understand and resolve issues effectively.

5. Handling Informational and Redirect Responses: Although less common, it is still important to handle informational and

redirect responses appropriately. Informational responses may require additional actions or processing, while redirect responses may require your application to follow the new location and perform the request again.

6. Implementing Retry and Circuit Breaker Patterns: In some cases, API requests may fail due to temporary issues, such as network connectivity problems or server overload. Implementing retry and circuit breaker patterns can help improve the resilience of your application by automatically retrying failed requests or temporarily stopping requests to a failing API.

By following these best practices, you can ensure that your C# and .NET applications handle API responses effectively, providing a seamless user experience and robust error handling capabilities.

7.4.3 Implementing Error Handling

Error handling is a critical aspect of building robust and reliable business applications. When working with web APIs, it is essential to implement a comprehensive error handling mechanism to handle various types of errors that may occur during API interactions. Here are some best practices for implementing error handling in your C# and .NET applications:

1. Centralized Error Handling: Implement a centralized error handling mechanism that captures and handles errors consistently across your application. This approach helps avoid code duplication and ensures that all errors are handled uniformly.

2. Logging Errors: Logging errors is crucial for troubleshooting and debugging purposes. Implement a logging mechanism that captures relevant error information, such as error messages, stack traces, and request details. Use a logging

framework like Serilog or log4net to simplify the logging process.

3. Providing User-Friendly Error Messages: When an error occurs, it is important to provide meaningful and user-friendly error messages to the end-users. Avoid exposing technical details or sensitive information in error messages. Instead, provide clear instructions or suggestions on how to resolve the issue or contact support.

4. Error Recovery and Retry: Depending on the nature of the error, you may implement error recovery mechanisms to handle specific types of errors automatically. For example, if an API request fails due to a temporary network issue, you can retry the request after a short delay. Implementing retry logic can help improve the reliability of your application.

5. Graceful Degradation: In some cases, an API may become temporarily unavailable or return errors due to maintenance or other issues. Implement graceful degradation mechanisms that allow your application to continue functioning with limited functionality or fallback options when the API is unavailable.

6. Custom Error Handling Middleware: In web applications, you can implement custom error handling middleware to intercept and handle errors at the application level. This middleware can capture unhandled exceptions, log them, and return appropriate error responses to the client.

By implementing these error handling best practices, you can ensure that your C# and .NET applications handle errors effectively, provide meaningful feedback to users, and maintain the overall stability and reliability of your business applications.

Conclusion

In this section, we explored the importance of working with API responses and implementing robust error handling mechanisms in your C# and .NET applications. We discussed the different types of API responses and provided best practices for handling them effectively. Additionally, we covered the implementation of error handling mechanisms to ensure that your applications can handle various types of errors gracefully. By following these best practices, you can build business applications that seamlessly integrate with web APIs and provide a reliable and user-friendly experience.

8 - Testing and Debugging Best Practices

8.1 Importance of Testing and Debugging

Testing and debugging are crucial aspects of software development that ensure the quality and reliability of business applications. These processes help identify and fix errors, validate functionality, and optimize performance. By investing time and effort into testing and debugging, developers can deliver robust and reliable applications that meet the needs of users and stakeholders. In this section, we will explore the importance of testing and debugging in the context of building business apps in C# and .NET.

8.1.1 Ensuring Application Reliability

One of the primary goals of testing and debugging is to ensure the reliability of the application. By thoroughly testing the codebase, developers can identify and fix any issues or bugs that may arise during the execution of the application. This helps prevent unexpected crashes, data corruption, or incorrect behavior that could negatively impact the user experience. Through rigorous testing, developers can gain confidence in the stability and reliability of their applications.

8.1.2 Validating Functionality

Testing and debugging also play a crucial role in validating the functionality of the application. Through various testing techniques such as unit testing, integration testing, and system testing, developers can verify that the application behaves as expected and meets the specified requirements. This ensures that the application performs the intended tasks accurately and consistently, providing users with a seamless experience. By identifying and addressing any functional issues early in the development process, developers can avoid costly rework and improve overall productivity.

8.1.3 Identifying and Fixing Errors

Errors and bugs are inevitable in software development. Testing and debugging provide developers with the means to identify and fix these issues effectively. Through systematic testing, developers can uncover errors in the codebase, such as logic flaws, data inconsistencies, or performance bottlenecks. Debugging techniques, such as stepping through code and using breakpoints, allow developers to pinpoint the root cause of the issue and apply the necessary fixes. By addressing errors promptly, developers can enhance the stability and performance of the application.

8.1.4 Optimizing Performance

Testing and debugging are not only about finding and fixing errors but also about optimizing the performance of the application. Through performance testing, developers can identify areas of the code that may cause performance degradation, such as inefficient algorithms or resource-intensive operations. By analyzing and optimizing these areas, developers can enhance the overall performance and responsiveness of the application. This ensures that the application can handle the expected workload efficiently, providing a smooth user experience.

8.1.5 Ensuring Compatibility and Scalability

Testing and debugging also play a crucial role in ensuring compatibility and scalability of business applications. Compatibility testing helps verify that the application works correctly across different platforms, operating systems, and devices. This ensures that the application can reach a broader audience and cater to the diverse needs of users. Scalability testing, on the other hand, helps assess the application's ability to handle increasing workloads and user demands. By testing the application under various load conditions, developers can identify and address any scalability issues, ensuring that the application can grow and adapt to changing business requirements.

8.1.6 Enhancing User Experience

Ultimately, testing and debugging contribute to enhancing the overall user experience of business applications. By thoroughly testing the application's functionality, reliability, and performance, developers can deliver a high-quality product that meets the expectations of users. This helps build trust and loyalty among users, leading to increased user satisfaction and engagement. Additionally, by promptly addressing any issues or bugs through debugging, developers can provide a seamless and error-free experience to users, ensuring their continued usage and adoption of the application.

In conclusion, testing and debugging are essential components of the software development process, especially when building business applications in C# and .NET. By investing time and effort into testing and debugging, developers can ensure the reliability, functionality, and performance of their applications. This leads to enhanced user experience, increased user satisfaction, and improved business outcomes. In the next section, we will explore specific techniques and best practices for unit testing business logic and components.

8.2 Unit Testing Business Logic and Components

Unit testing is an essential part of software development as it helps ensure the quality and reliability of your code. By testing individual units of code, such as functions or methods, you can identify and fix bugs early in the development process. In this section, we will explore the importance of unit testing in building business apps and discuss best practices for testing business logic and components.

8.2.1 Understanding the Importance of Unit Testing

Unit testing plays a crucial role in the development of business apps. It allows you to verify that each unit of code, such as a function or method, behaves as expected and produces the correct output for a given input. By writing tests for your business logic and components, you can catch bugs and issues before they impact the overall functionality of your application.

Unit testing provides several benefits, including:

1. **Early bug detection**: By writing tests before implementing the actual code, you can identify and fix issues early in the development process. This helps prevent bugs from propagating to other parts of the application.

2. **Improved code quality**: Writing tests forces you to think about the expected behavior of your code and ensures that it meets the specified requirements. This leads to cleaner and more maintainable code.

3. **Regression testing**: Unit tests act as a safety net when making changes to your codebase. By running tests after making modifications, you can quickly identify any regressions or unintended side effects.

4. **Documentation**: Unit tests serve as living documentation for

your codebase. They provide examples of how to use your business logic and components and can help new developers understand the expected behavior.

8.2.2 Writing Unit Tests for Business Logic

When writing unit tests for business logic, it is essential to focus on testing individual units of code in isolation. This means that you should test each function or method independently, without relying on external dependencies such as databases or APIs. By isolating the code being tested, you can ensure that any failures are due to issues within the unit itself and not caused by external factors.

To write effective unit tests for your business logic, follow these best practices:

1. **Test one thing at a time**: Each unit test should focus on testing a single aspect of your business logic. This allows for better isolation and makes it easier to identify the cause of failures.

2. **Use meaningful test names**: Give your tests descriptive names that clearly indicate what aspect of the business logic they are testing. This makes it easier to understand the purpose of each test and helps with debugging.

3. **Cover edge cases**: Ensure that your tests cover a range of input values, including boundary cases and invalid inputs. This helps uncover potential issues and ensures that your business logic handles all scenarios correctly.

4. **Mock external dependencies**: When testing business logic that relies on external dependencies, such as databases or APIs, use mocking frameworks to simulate their behavior. This allows you to control the responses and focus solely on testing the logic within your unit.

5. **Follow the Arrange-Act-Assert pattern**: Structure your tests

using the Arrange-Act-Assert pattern. In the Arrange phase, set up the necessary preconditions for the test. In the Act phase, execute the code being tested. Finally, in the Assert phase, verify that the output matches the expected result.

8.2.3 Testing Components and Integration Points

In addition to testing business logic, it is crucial to test the integration points and components that make up your application. This includes testing interactions with databases, APIs, and other external systems. Integration testing ensures that these components work correctly together and that the application behaves as expected in a real-world environment.

When testing components and integration points, consider the following best practices:

1. **Use a separate test environment**: Set up a separate environment for integration testing to avoid interfering with the production system. This allows you to test against real databases, APIs, and other external systems without affecting live data.

2. **Automate the setup and teardown**: Automate the setup and teardown of the test environment to ensure consistency and repeatability. This includes creating and populating test databases, starting and stopping services, and resetting any external systems.

3. **Test different scenarios**: Test various scenarios to ensure that your application handles different inputs and conditions correctly. This includes testing error handling, edge cases, and performance under load.

4. **Monitor and log**: Monitor and log the behavior of your application during integration testing. This helps identify any issues or performance bottlenecks and provides valuable

insights for debugging.

8.2.4 Choosing a Unit Testing Framework

There are several unit testing frameworks available for C# and .NET development. Some popular options include:

1. **NUnit**: NUnit is a widely used unit testing framework for .NET. It provides a rich set of features for writing and executing tests, including support for parameterized tests, test fixtures, and assertions.

2. **xUnit.net**: xUnit.net is another popular unit testing framework that follows a similar syntax to NUnit. It offers a clean and extensible architecture and supports parallel test execution.

3. **Microsoft Unit Testing Framework**: The Microsoft Unit Testing Framework, also known as MSTest, is the default testing framework included with Visual Studio. It provides a simple and intuitive way to write and execute tests.

When choosing a unit testing framework, consider factors such as community support, integration with your development environment, and the specific features and capabilities you require.

Conclusion

Unit testing is a critical aspect of building business apps in C# and .NET. By writing tests for your business logic and components, you can ensure the quality and reliability of your code. Follow best practices for writing effective unit tests, including isolating the code being tested, covering edge cases, and using meaningful test names. Additionally, test the integration points and components of your application to ensure that they work correctly together. Choose a unit testing framework that best suits your needs and integrate it into your development workflow.

8.3 Debugging Techniques and Tools

Debugging is an essential part of software development. It allows developers to identify and fix issues in their code, ensuring that the application functions as intended. In this section, we will explore various debugging techniques and tools available in C# and .NET to help you effectively debug your business applications.

8.3.1 Understanding the Importance of Debugging

Debugging is the process of identifying and resolving errors, bugs, and other issues in software. It plays a crucial role in ensuring the quality and reliability of your business applications. By debugging your code, you can:

- Identify and fix logical errors: Debugging helps you identify and fix logical errors in your code that may cause unexpected behavior or incorrect results.
- Trace program flow: Debugging allows you to trace the flow of your program, step by step, to understand how it executes and identify any issues along the way.
- Inspect variables and data: Debugging tools provide the ability to inspect the values of variables and data structures at runtime, helping you understand how they change and identify any inconsistencies.
- Test and validate code changes: Debugging allows you to test and validate code changes before deploying them, ensuring that they work as expected and do not introduce new issues.

8.3.2 Debugging Techniques

When it comes to debugging, there are several techniques you can employ to effectively identify and resolve issues in your code. Let's explore some of these techniques:

8.3.2.1 Setting Breakpoints

One of the most common debugging techniques is setting breakpoints in your code. A breakpoint is a marker that tells the debugger to pause the execution of the program at a specific line of code. By setting breakpoints at strategic locations, you can examine the state of your program and variables at that point in time.

To set a breakpoint in Visual Studio, simply click on the left margin of the code editor window at the desired line of code. When the program reaches the breakpoint, it will pause, allowing you to inspect variables, step through the code, and analyze the program's behavior.

8.3.2.2 Stepping Through Code

Stepping through code is another useful debugging technique. It allows you to execute your program line by line, observing how the variables and data change at each step. This technique is particularly helpful when trying to understand the flow of your program or identify issues in complex logic.

In Visual Studio, you can step through your code using the following commands:

- Step Into (F11): This command allows you to step into a method or function call, allowing you to examine the code inside that method.
- Step Over (F10): This command allows you to execute the current line of code and move to the next line without

stepping into any method or function calls.

- Step Out (Shift + F11): This command allows you to step out of the current method or function and return to the calling code.

8.3.2.3 Debugging with Conditional Breakpoints

Conditional breakpoints are breakpoints that are triggered only when a specific condition is met. This technique is useful when you want to pause the execution of your program only when a certain condition is true.

To set a conditional breakpoint in Visual Studio, right-click on an existing breakpoint and select "Condition." Then, enter the condition that you want to evaluate. When the program reaches the breakpoint, it will only pause if the condition is true.

8.3.2.4 Logging and Debug Output

Logging and debug output are essential techniques for debugging applications, especially in production environments where attaching a debugger may not be feasible. By strategically placing log statements or using the debug output window, you can output relevant information about the state of your application, variable values, and error messages.

In C#, you can use the Debug class to write debug output messages. These messages can be viewed in the "Output" window in Visual Studio or captured in log files for later analysis.

8.3.3 Debugging Tools

In addition to the debugging techniques mentioned above, there are several powerful debugging tools available in C# and .NET that can greatly enhance your debugging experience. Let's explore some of these tools:

8.3.3.1 Visual Studio Debugger

Visual Studio provides a robust and feature-rich debugger that allows you to debug your C# and .NET applications effectively. It offers a wide range of debugging features, including breakpoints, step-through debugging, watch windows, call stack analysis, and more.

The Visual Studio debugger also supports advanced features like multi-threaded debugging, remote debugging, and debugging of web applications. It provides a comprehensive set of tools and features to help you identify and resolve issues in your code efficiently.

8.3.3.2 Profiling Tools

Profiling tools are used to analyze the performance of your application and identify areas that can be optimized. These tools provide insights into CPU usage, memory allocation, and other performance metrics, helping you identify bottlenecks and optimize your code.

Visual Studio includes a built-in profiling tool called the "Performance Profiler." This tool allows you to collect performance data, analyze it, and identify performance issues in your application. It provides various profiling modes, such as CPU sampling, memory profiling, and concurrency profiling, to help you optimize your code for better performance.

8.3.3.3 Third-Party Debugging Tools

In addition to the built-in debugging tools in Visual Studio, there are also several third-party debugging tools available that can enhance your debugging experience. These tools offer additional features and capabilities that can help you debug complex applications more effectively.

Some popular third-party debugging tools for C# and .NET include JetBrains dotTrace, Redgate ANTS Performance Profiler, and Telerik JustTrace. These tools provide advanced debugging and profiling features, such as memory and performance analysis, code coverage, and more.

Conclusion

Debugging is an essential skill for every software developer. By understanding the importance of debugging and employing effective debugging techniques and tools, you can identify and resolve issues in your business applications efficiently. The Visual Studio debugger, along with profiling tools and third-party debugging tools, provides a comprehensive set of features to help you debug and optimize your code.

8.4 Performance Testing and Optimization

Performance testing and optimization are crucial steps in the development process of any business application. As your application grows and handles more data and users, it is essential to ensure that it performs efficiently and meets the performance requirements of your users. In this section, we will explore the importance of performance testing, techniques for measuring performance, and strategies for optimizing the performance of your C# and .NET business applications.

8.4.1 Importance of Performance Testing

Performance testing is the process of evaluating the speed, responsiveness, stability, and scalability of an application under various workload conditions. It helps identify bottlenecks, performance issues, and areas for improvement. By conducting performance testing, you can ensure that your application meets the performance expectations of your users and provides a smooth and responsive user experience.

There are several reasons why performance testing is crucial for your business applications:

1. **User Satisfaction**: Users expect applications to respond quickly and provide a seamless experience. Performance testing helps identify and resolve any performance-related issues that may impact user satisfaction.
2. **Scalability**: As your application grows, it needs to handle an increasing number of users and data. Performance testing helps determine the scalability of your application and ensures that it can handle the expected load.
3. **Efficient Resource Utilization**: Performance testing helps identify resource-intensive areas in your application, such as memory leaks or excessive CPU usage. By optimizing these

areas, you can ensure efficient resource utilization and reduce infrastructure costs.

4. **Competitive Advantage**: In today's competitive market, performance can be a differentiating factor. A well-performing application can attract and retain users, giving your business a competitive edge.

8.4.2 Measuring Performance

Before optimizing the performance of your application, it is essential to measure its current performance. This allows you to identify the areas that require improvement and set performance goals. Here are some common techniques for measuring performance:

1. **Response Time**: Response time measures the time taken by the application to respond to a user request. It is a critical metric for evaluating the user experience. You can measure response time using tools like performance profilers or by adding logging statements in your code.

2. **Throughput**: Throughput measures the number of transactions or requests processed by the application per unit of time. It helps evaluate the application's capacity to handle a specific workload. You can measure throughput by simulating a realistic workload and monitoring the number of requests processed.

3. **Concurrency**: Concurrency measures the application's ability to handle multiple simultaneous requests. It is essential to ensure that your application can handle concurrent users without performance degradation. You can measure concurrency by simulating concurrent user scenarios and monitoring the application's response time.

4. **Resource Utilization**: Resource utilization measures the application's consumption of system resources such as CPU,

memory, and disk I/O. Monitoring resource utilization helps identify resource-intensive areas that may impact performance. You can use performance monitoring tools or built-in performance counters in Windows to measure resource utilization.

8.4.3 Performance Optimization Strategies

Once you have identified the performance bottlenecks in your application, you can start optimizing its performance. Here are some strategies for performance optimization:

1. **Code Optimization**: Review your code for any inefficient algorithms, unnecessary database queries, or resource-intensive operations. Optimize your code by using efficient data structures, caching, and minimizing database round trips.

2. **Database Optimization**: Analyze your database queries and optimize them for better performance. Use indexing, query optimization techniques, and stored procedures to improve database performance. Consider denormalizing data or implementing caching mechanisms to reduce database load.

3. **Caching**: Implement caching mechanisms to store frequently accessed data in memory. Caching can significantly improve application performance by reducing the need for expensive database queries or calculations.

4. **Asynchronous Programming**: Utilize asynchronous programming techniques to improve the responsiveness of your application. Asynchronous programming allows your application to perform multiple tasks concurrently, reducing the overall response time.

5. **Load Balancing**: If your application is deployed in a distributed environment, consider implementing load balancing to distribute the workload across multiple servers.

Load balancing helps improve performance and ensures high availability.

6. **Optimized Network Communication**: Optimize network communication by minimizing the size of data transferred, reducing the number of round trips, and utilizing compression techniques. Efficient network communication can significantly improve application performance, especially in distributed systems.

7. **Performance Testing and Monitoring**: Continuously perform performance testing and monitoring to identify any new performance issues and ensure that your optimizations are effective. Regularly monitor key performance metrics and address any performance degradation promptly.

Remember, performance optimization is an iterative process. Continuously monitor and analyze the performance of your application, identify areas for improvement, and implement optimizations accordingly.

By following these performance testing and optimization strategies, you can ensure that your C# and .NET business applications deliver optimal performance, meet user expectations, and provide a seamless user experience.

Conclusion

In this section, we explored the importance of performance testing and optimization in building business applications. We discussed the significance of performance testing, techniques for measuring performance, and strategies for optimizing application performance. By incorporating performance testing and optimization into your development process, you can ensure that your applications perform efficiently, meet user expectations, and provide a competitive advantage in the market. In the next section, we will delve into the topic of deploying updates and managing versions in business applications.

9 - Deploying Updates and Managing Versions

9.1 Introduction to Deployment and Versioning

In the software development lifecycle, deployment and versioning play a crucial role in ensuring that applications are successfully released and maintained. Deployment refers to the process of making an application available for use, while versioning involves managing different iterations or releases of the application. This chapter will provide you with an understanding of deployment and versioning concepts and guide you through the implementation of continuous integration and deployment, managing application versions and updates, as well as rollback strategies and disaster recovery.

9.1.1 Understanding Deployment

Deployment is the process of taking a developed application and making it available for users to access and utilize. It involves a series of steps to ensure that the application is installed, configured, and ready to run on the target environment. Successful deployment is crucial for delivering a reliable and functional application to end-users.

During the deployment process, various aspects need to be considered, such as the target platform, dependencies, configuration settings, and security requirements. It is essential to have a well-defined deployment strategy to ensure a smooth and error-free deployment experience.

9.1.2 Introduction to Versioning

Versioning is the practice of assigning unique identifiers to different iterations or releases of an application. It allows developers and users to track changes, manage updates, and ensure compatibility between different versions of the application. Versioning is crucial for maintaining and evolving software applications over time.

A version number typically consists of a series of numbers or alphanumeric characters separated by dots. Each segment of the version number represents a different level of change, such as major, minor, or patch updates. For example, a version number of "1.2.3" might indicate a major release, a minor feature update, and a bug fix, respectively.

Versioning enables developers to communicate changes effectively, manage dependencies, and provide users with a clear understanding of the application's evolution. It also facilitates the implementation of update strategies, such as rolling out new features or bug fixes while ensuring backward compatibility.

9.1.3 Implementing Continuous Integration and Deployment

Continuous Integration (CI) and Continuous Deployment (CD) are practices that aim to automate the process of building, testing, and deploying applications. CI involves regularly integrating code changes from multiple developers into a shared repository, while CD focuses on automating the deployment of these changes to production environments.

Implementing CI/CD pipelines can significantly improve the efficiency and reliability of the deployment process. It allows developers to catch integration issues early, automate testing, and ensure that the application is always in a deployable state. CI/CD pipelines also enable frequent and incremental deployments, reducing the risk associated with large-scale releases.

To implement CI/CD, you can leverage various tools and technologies, such as build servers, version control systems, and deployment automation frameworks. Popular tools like Jenkins, Azure

DevOps, and GitHub Actions provide robust CI/CD capabilities and can be integrated into your development workflow.

9.1.4 Managing Application Versions and Updates

Managing application versions and updates is crucial for maintaining and evolving software applications. It involves tracking different releases, managing dependencies, and ensuring a smooth transition for users when updating to a new version.

One common approach to managing application versions is to use version control systems like Git. Version control systems allow you to track changes, create branches for different features or bug fixes, and merge them back into the main codebase. By tagging specific commits or branches, you can create distinct versions of your application.

When releasing a new version, it is essential to communicate the changes effectively to users. This can be done through release notes, documentation, or even in-app notifications. Providing clear instructions and highlighting new features or bug fixes helps users understand the value of the update and encourages them to adopt the latest version.

9.1.5 Rollback Strategies and Disaster Recovery

Despite careful planning and testing, issues may arise during the deployment process or after an update. Rollback strategies and disaster recovery plans are essential to mitigate the impact of such issues and ensure business continuity.

A rollback strategy involves reverting to a previous version of the application in case of critical failures or issues. By keeping backups of previous versions and having a well-defined rollback process, you can quickly restore the application to a stable state. It is crucial to test rollback procedures in advance to ensure their effectiveness.

Disaster recovery plans go beyond simple rollbacks and address more severe incidents, such as infrastructure failures or data breaches.

These plans outline the steps to recover the application and its data in the event of a disaster. They may include backup and restore procedures, failover mechanisms, and communication protocols to notify stakeholders about the incident.

By implementing robust rollback strategies and disaster recovery plans, you can minimize the impact of unforeseen issues and ensure the availability and reliability of your application.

Conclusion

Deployment and versioning are critical aspects of the software development lifecycle. Understanding the deployment process, implementing versioning strategies, and having robust CI/CD pipelines are essential for successful application releases. Additionally, managing application versions, communicating updates effectively, and planning for rollbacks and disaster recovery contribute to maintaining a reliable and resilient application. By following the best practices outlined in this chapter, you will be well-equipped to deploy and manage your business applications effectively.

9.2 Implementing Continuous Integration and Deployment

Continuous Integration (CI) and Continuous Deployment (CD) are essential practices in modern software development. They enable teams to automate the process of building, testing, and deploying applications, ensuring that changes are integrated smoothly and efficiently. In this section, we will explore the steps involved in implementing CI/CD for your business applications built in C# and .NET.

9.2.1 Setting up a CI/CD Pipeline

To implement CI/CD, you need to set up a pipeline that automates the build, test, and deployment processes. Here are the steps involved:

1. Version Control: Use a version control system like Git to manage your source code. Create a repository for your application and ensure that all team members commit their changes regularly.

2. Build Automation: Use a build automation tool like Jenkins or Azure DevOps to automate the build process. Configure the build tool to fetch the latest code from the repository, compile it, and generate the necessary artifacts.

3. Automated Testing: Implement a comprehensive suite of automated tests to ensure the quality of your application. Include unit tests, integration tests, and end-to-end tests. Configure the build tool to run these tests automatically after the build process.

4. Code Analysis: Integrate a code analysis tool like SonarQube or ReSharper into your CI/CD pipeline. This tool will analyze your code for potential issues, such as code smells, security vulnerabilities, and performance bottlenecks.

Configure the build tool to generate reports based on the code analysis results.

5. Artifact Repository: Set up an artifact repository to store the build artifacts generated by the build tool. This repository will serve as a centralized location for storing and managing your application's deployable packages.

6. Deployment Automation: Use a deployment automation tool like Octopus Deploy or Azure DevOps to automate the deployment process. Configure the deployment tool to fetch the latest build artifacts from the artifact repository and deploy them to the target environment.

7. Environment Configuration: Define different environments for your application, such as development, testing, staging, and production. Configure the deployment tool to deploy the application to the appropriate environment based on the deployment stage.

8. Continuous Monitoring: Implement a monitoring solution to track the performance and availability of your application. Configure the monitoring tool to send alerts in case of any issues or anomalies.

9.2.2 Best Practices for CI/CD

Implementing CI/CD requires following certain best practices to ensure the smooth functioning of the pipeline. Here are some key practices to consider:

1. Automated Builds: Ensure that the build process is fully automated and can be triggered with a single command or commit. This reduces the chances of human error and ensures consistency across builds.

2. Versioning: Use a versioning scheme to track different versions of your application. This helps in identifying and

rolling back to specific versions if needed.

3. Branching Strategy: Define a branching strategy that suits your development workflow. Use branches to isolate new features, bug fixes, and hotfixes. Merge branches into the main branch (e.g., master) after they have been tested and reviewed.

4. Continuous Testing: Implement a comprehensive suite of automated tests that cover different aspects of your application. Run these tests as part of the CI/CD pipeline to catch any issues early in the development process.

5. Infrastructure as Code: Use infrastructure as code (IaC) tools like Terraform or Azure Resource Manager to define and manage your application's infrastructure. This ensures that the infrastructure is consistent across different environments and can be easily reproduced.

6. Rollback Strategy: Define a rollback strategy to handle situations where a deployment fails or causes issues in the production environment. This strategy should include steps to revert to the previous version and investigate the cause of the failure.

7. Continuous Feedback: Implement mechanisms to provide continuous feedback to the development team. This can include automated reports, notifications, and dashboards that highlight the status of the CI/CD pipeline and any issues that need attention.

9.2.3 Continuous Integration and Deployment Tools

There are several tools available for implementing CI/CD for your C# and .NET applications. Here are some popular ones:

1. Jenkins: An open-source automation server that supports building, testing, and deploying applications.

2. Azure DevOps: A cloud-based platform that provides a

complete set of tools for CI/CD, including source control, build automation, testing, and deployment.

3. Octopus Deploy: A deployment automation tool that simplifies the process of deploying applications to different environments.

4. TeamCity: A powerful CI/CD server that supports building, testing, and deploying applications across different platforms.

5. GitLab CI/CD: A built-in CI/CD solution provided by GitLab, a web-based Git repository manager.

Choose a tool that best fits your requirements and integrates well with your existing development workflow.

Implementing CI/CD for your business applications in C# and .NET can significantly improve the efficiency and reliability of your development process. By automating the build, test, and deployment processes, you can ensure that changes are integrated smoothly and deployed to production with confidence. Follow the best practices outlined in this section and leverage the available tools to set up a robust CI/CD pipeline for your applications.

9.3 Managing Application Versions and Updates

Managing application versions and updates is a critical aspect of software development and deployment. As your business application evolves and grows, you will inevitably need to release updates to address bugs, add new features, and improve performance. In this section, we will explore best practices for managing application versions and updates to ensure a smooth and seamless experience for your users.

9.3.1 Versioning Your Application

Versioning your application is essential for tracking changes and ensuring compatibility between different releases. By assigning a unique version number to each release, you can easily identify and manage different versions of your application. There are different versioning schemes you can use, such as semantic versioning (e.g., MAJOR.MINOR.PATCH) or date-based versioning.

When choosing a versioning scheme, consider the needs of your application and your users. Semantic versioning is a popular choice as it provides a clear indication of the significance of each release. It consists of three components:

1. MAJOR version: Incremented when you make incompatible changes or introduce significant new features.
2. MINOR version: Incremented when you add functionality in a backward-compatible manner.
3. PATCH version: Incremented when you make backward-compatible bug fixes.

Additionally, you can include pre-release and build metadata in your versioning scheme to indicate development stages or specific builds.

9.3.2 Release Management

Effective release management is crucial for delivering updates to your users efficiently. It involves planning, coordinating, and executing the release process to ensure a smooth transition from one version to another. Here are some key steps to consider:

1. Release Planning: Define a release schedule and prioritize the features and bug fixes to be included in each release. Consider the impact of each change and plan accordingly.
2. Version Control: Use a version control system, such as Git, to manage your source code and track changes. Create branches for each release and use tags to mark specific versions.
3. Continuous Integration and Deployment: Implement a CI/ CD pipeline to automate the build, testing, and deployment process. This ensures that each release is thoroughly tested and can be deployed with minimal manual intervention.
4. Release Notes: Prepare release notes that document the changes, bug fixes, and new features included in each release. This helps users understand what to expect and provides a reference for troubleshooting.
5. User Communication: Notify your users about upcoming releases and inform them of any changes or new features. Provide clear instructions on how to update their applications and address any potential concerns or compatibility issues.

9.3.3 Update Distribution

Once you have prepared a new release, you need to distribute it to your users. There are several methods you can use to distribute updates, depending on the nature of your application and your users' preferences:

1. Automatic Updates: Implement an automatic update

mechanism within your application that checks for updates and downloads them in the background. This ensures that users always have the latest version without manual intervention.

2. Manual Updates: Provide a download link on your website or within your application for users to manually download and install updates. This method gives users more control over the update process but requires them to actively check for updates.

3. App Stores: If your application is available on app stores like Microsoft Store or Apple App Store, you can distribute updates through these platforms. Users can receive notifications and easily update their applications with a few clicks.

4. Enterprise Deployment: If your application is used within an enterprise environment, consider working with IT departments to distribute updates through centralized deployment tools like Microsoft System Center Configuration Manager (SCCM) or Group Policy.

Regardless of the distribution method, it is essential to ensure that the update process is seamless and user-friendly. Provide clear instructions, minimize downtime during the update, and handle any potential conflicts or compatibility issues gracefully.

9.3.4 Rollback Strategies and Disaster Recovery

Despite careful planning and testing, there may be instances where an update introduces unforeseen issues or compatibility problems. In such cases, having a rollback strategy and disaster recovery plan is crucial to minimize the impact on your users and business operations.

1. Rollback Strategy: Define a rollback strategy that allows you to revert to a previous version quickly. This may involve

keeping backups of previous releases, maintaining a separate environment for testing updates, or using feature toggles to enable/disable specific functionality.

2. Monitoring and Feedback: Implement monitoring tools to track the performance and stability of your application after an update. Encourage users to provide feedback and promptly address any issues that arise.

3. Disaster Recovery Plan: Prepare a disaster recovery plan that outlines the steps to be taken in the event of a catastrophic failure or data loss. This may involve regular backups, redundant infrastructure, and a clear process for restoring services.

By having a well-defined rollback strategy and disaster recovery plan in place, you can mitigate the risks associated with updates and ensure that your application remains stable and reliable.

In conclusion, managing application versions and updates is a critical aspect of building business apps. By following best practices for versioning, release management, update distribution, and having a rollback strategy, you can ensure a smooth and seamless experience for your users while maintaining the stability and reliability of your application.

9.4 Rollback Strategies and Disaster Recovery

In the world of software development, it is crucial to have a plan in place for handling unforeseen issues and disasters that may occur during the deployment and management of business applications. Rollback strategies and disaster recovery plans are essential components of any robust and reliable system. In this section, we will explore the importance of rollback strategies and disaster recovery, and discuss best practices for implementing them in your C# and .NET business applications.

9.4.1 Understanding Rollback Strategies

A rollback strategy is a predefined plan that outlines the steps to be taken in the event of a failed deployment or update. It allows you to revert to a previous version of your application, ensuring that your system remains functional and stable. Rollback strategies are particularly important when deploying updates to production environments, as they provide a safety net in case something goes wrong.

When designing a rollback strategy, consider the following key aspects:

1. **Version Control**: Ensure that your application code is properly versioned using a version control system such as Git. This allows you to easily revert to a previous version if needed.

2. **Database Backups**: Regularly backup your application's database to ensure that you have a recent copy of your data. This will enable you to restore the database to a known good state in the event of a rollback.

3. **Automated Testing**: Implement a comprehensive suite of automated tests to validate the functionality of your application after each deployment. These tests should cover

critical business processes and ensure that the application is working as expected.

4. **Monitoring and Logging**: Implement robust monitoring and logging mechanisms to track the health and performance of your application. This will help you identify issues early on and take appropriate action.

9.4.2 Implementing Rollback Strategies

To implement a rollback strategy in your C# and .NET business application, follow these best practices:

1. **Automated Deployment Scripts**: Use automated deployment scripts, such as PowerShell or Azure DevOps, to ensure consistent and repeatable deployments. These scripts should include the necessary steps to rollback to a previous version if required.

2. **Feature Toggles**: Implement feature toggles in your application code to enable or disable specific features at runtime. This allows you to easily turn off a problematic feature in case of a rollback.

3. **Database Migrations**: Use database migration tools, such as Entity Framework Migrations, to manage changes to your database schema. These tools allow you to roll back database changes by applying previous migrations.

4. **Backup and Restore Procedures**: Establish backup and restore procedures for your application's database. Regularly backup the database and test the restore process to ensure that it works correctly.

5. **Rollback Testing**: Perform regular rollback testing to validate the effectiveness of your rollback strategy. This involves simulating a failed deployment and executing the rollback process to ensure that it restores the application to a stable

state.

9.4.3 Disaster Recovery Planning

In addition to rollback strategies, it is essential to have a disaster recovery plan in place to handle catastrophic events that may impact your business application. A disaster recovery plan outlines the steps to be taken in the event of a major system failure, such as hardware failure, natural disasters, or cyber-attacks.

When creating a disaster recovery plan, consider the following:

1. **Identify Critical Systems**: Identify the critical components and systems that are essential for the operation of your business application. This includes servers, databases, network infrastructure, and any third-party services.

2. **Backup and Replication**: Implement a robust backup and replication strategy to ensure that your critical systems are replicated to a secondary location. This allows for quick recovery in the event of a disaster.

3. **Redundancy and Failover**: Design your infrastructure with redundancy and failover capabilities to minimize downtime. This may involve using load balancers, clustering, or virtualization technologies.

4. **Regular Testing**: Regularly test your disaster recovery plan to ensure that it is effective and up to date. This includes performing simulated disaster scenarios and validating the recovery process.

5. **Communication and Documentation**: Establish clear communication channels and document the disaster recovery plan. Ensure that all stakeholders are aware of their roles and responsibilities in the event of a disaster.

9.4.4 Business Continuity

Rollback strategies and disaster recovery plans are essential for maintaining business continuity. By having these plans in place, you can minimize downtime, reduce the impact of failures, and ensure that your business applications are always available to users.

Remember that rollback strategies and disaster recovery plans should be regularly reviewed and updated as your application evolves. As new features are added and infrastructure changes, it is important to ensure that your plans remain relevant and effective.

In conclusion, implementing rollback strategies and disaster recovery plans are critical for the success of your C# and .NET business applications. By following best practices and regularly testing these plans, you can ensure that your applications remain resilient and reliable, even in the face of unexpected challenges.

10 - Building Common Business Features

10.1 Order Processing and Management

Order processing and management is a critical aspect of any business application. It involves the handling of customer orders, tracking their progress, managing inventory, and ensuring timely delivery. In this section, we will explore the step-by-step process of building order processing and management functionality in a C# and .NET business application.

10.1.1 Designing the Order Data Model

Before we can start implementing order processing and management, we need to design the data model that will store and represent order-related information. This includes entities such as customers, products, orders, and order items. We will use a relational database, such as SQL Server, to store this data.

To design the order data model, we need to consider the relationships between these entities. For example, a customer can have multiple orders, and each order can have multiple order items. We will use Entity Framework, an ORM framework, to map these relationships to our database tables.

10.1.2 Creating the Order User Interface

The next step is to design the user interface for order processing and management. We will use Windows Forms to create a user-friendly interface that allows users to view, create, update, and delete orders. The UI should provide a clear and intuitive way for users to navigate through the application and perform order-related tasks.

The order user interface should include features such as:

- A dashboard or summary view displaying key order metrics and statistics.
- A search functionality to find orders based on various criteria such as customer name, order date, or order status.
- A form for creating new orders, including the ability to select products and specify quantities.
- An order details view showing all the information related to a specific order, including customer details, order items, and order status.
- The ability to update and delete orders, as well as change the status of an order (e.g., from "pending" to "shipped").

10.1.3 Implementing Order Processing Logic

Once we have the data model and user interface in place, we can start implementing the order processing logic. This involves writing code to handle various order-related operations, such as creating new orders, updating existing orders, and managing order status.

We will implement business rules and workflows to enforce order processing rules, such as ensuring that all required fields are filled, validating order quantities against available inventory, and calculating order totals. We will also handle exceptions and errors that may occur during order processing, providing appropriate error messages and feedback to the user.

10.1.4 Integrating with Inventory Management

Order processing and management are closely tied to inventory management. When a customer places an order, we need to ensure that the ordered products are available in the inventory. If not, we should prevent the order from being processed or provide alternative options to the customer.

To integrate with inventory management, we will establish a connection between the order processing module and the inventory module of our application. This integration will allow us to check the availability of products, update inventory quantities when orders are processed, and generate alerts when inventory levels are low.

10.1.5 Generating Order Reports

Reporting is an essential aspect of order processing and management. It allows us to analyze order data, track performance, and make informed business decisions. In this step, we will generate reports that provide insights into order trends, customer behavior, and order fulfillment efficiency.

We can use RDLC (Report Definition Language Client) or third-party reporting libraries, such as Crystal Reports or Telerik Reporting, to design and generate order reports. These reports can include information such as order summaries, sales charts, top-selling products, and order fulfillment statistics.

10.1.6 Enhancing Order Processing with Automation

To streamline the order processing and management workflow, we can enhance the application with automation features. For example, we can implement automatic order confirmation emails to customers, order status updates, and notifications to the relevant departments when specific events occur (e.g., low inventory levels or delayed shipments).

By automating certain aspects of order processing, we can improve efficiency, reduce manual errors, and provide a better customer experience.

Conclusion

In this section, we have explored the step-by-step process of building order processing and management functionality in a C# and .NET business application. We started by designing the order data model, creating the user interface, and implementing the order processing logic. We also integrated with inventory management, generated order reports, and enhanced the workflow with automation. By following these steps, you can build a robust and efficient order processing and management system for your business application.

10.2 Inventory Management

Inventory management is a crucial aspect of any business that deals with physical products. It involves the tracking, control, and optimization of a company's inventory to ensure efficient operations and customer satisfaction. In this section, we will explore the key components and steps involved in building an inventory management system as part of a business application using C# and .NET.

10.2.1 Understanding Inventory Management

Before diving into the implementation details, it is essential to understand the fundamental concepts of inventory management. Inventory management encompasses various activities, including inventory tracking, stock control, order fulfillment, and demand forecasting. The primary goal is to maintain optimal inventory levels to meet customer demand while minimizing costs and maximizing profitability.

10.2.2 Designing the Inventory Data Model

The first step in building an inventory management system is designing the data model that represents the inventory and related entities. This includes defining entities such as products, suppliers, warehouses, and inventory transactions. Considerations should be given to capturing essential information such as product details, stock levels, reorder points, and supplier information.

10.2.3 Implementing Inventory Tracking

Inventory tracking involves keeping a real-time record of the quantity and location of each product in the inventory. This can be achieved by implementing functionality to track stock levels, receive new stock, and update stock quantities when products are sold or returned. Utilizing a database management system, such as SQL Server, can provide a robust foundation for storing and managing inventory data.

10.2.4 Managing Stock Control

Stock control is a critical aspect of inventory management that ensures optimal stock levels are maintained. This involves setting reorder points, safety stock levels, and implementing mechanisms to generate purchase orders or alerts when stock levels fall below the desired thresholds. By automating these processes, businesses can avoid stockouts and overstock situations, leading to improved efficiency and cost savings.

10.2.5 Fulfilling Orders and Managing Sales

An inventory management system should facilitate order fulfillment and sales management. This includes functionalities such as order processing, order picking, packing, and shipping. By integrating the inventory system with other components of the business application, such as the sales module, businesses can streamline the order fulfillment process and provide accurate information to customers regarding product availability and delivery times.

10.2.6 Reporting and Analytics

Reporting and analytics play a crucial role in inventory management, providing insights into inventory performance, demand patterns, and forecasting. By leveraging reporting tools such as RDLC or third-party libraries, businesses can generate comprehensive reports on inventory levels, stock turnover, and other key performance indicators. These reports can aid in decision-making, identifying trends, and optimizing inventory management strategies.

10.2.7 Integrating with Suppliers and Vendors

Efficient inventory management often involves collaboration with suppliers and vendors. Integrating the inventory management system with external systems or APIs can streamline processes such as supplier communication, purchase order generation, and receiving stock updates. By automating these interactions, businesses can reduce manual effort, improve accuracy, and enhance overall supply chain efficiency.

10.2.8 Implementing Inventory Optimization Techniques

Inventory optimization techniques aim to strike a balance between maintaining sufficient stock levels to meet customer demand and minimizing inventory holding costs. These techniques include demand forecasting, ABC analysis, economic order quantity (EOQ) calculations, and just-in-time (JIT) inventory management. By incorporating these techniques into the inventory management system, businesses can optimize inventory levels, reduce costs, and improve overall operational efficiency.

10.2.9 Enhancing Security and Access Control

As with any business application, security and access control are crucial considerations when building an inventory management system. Implementing user authentication, role-based access control, and data encryption can help protect sensitive inventory information from unauthorized access. Additionally, implementing audit trails and logging mechanisms can aid in tracking inventory-related activities and detecting any potential security breaches.

10.2.10 Testing and Maintenance

Thorough testing is essential to ensure the reliability and accuracy of the inventory management system. This includes unit testing individual components, integration testing, and end-to-end testing of the entire system. Additionally, regular maintenance and updates are necessary to address any bugs, performance issues, or changes in business requirements. Implementing automated testing and continuous integration practices can streamline the testing and maintenance processes.

In conclusion, building an inventory management system as part of a business application requires careful planning, design, and implementation. By following the steps outlined in this section, businesses can develop a robust and efficient inventory management system using C# and .NET, enabling them to optimize inventory levels, streamline operations, and enhance customer satisfaction.

10.3 HR Functions and Employee Management

In any organization, managing human resources is a critical aspect of running a successful business. HR functions involve various tasks such as employee recruitment, onboarding, performance management, and employee record-keeping. Building an efficient HR management system within your business application can streamline these processes and improve overall productivity. In this section, we will explore the key components and steps involved in building HR functions and employee management features in your C# and .NET business application.

10.3.1 Employee Data Model

Before diving into the implementation details, it is essential to design a robust data model to store employee information. The employee data model should capture relevant details such as personal information, job details, salary information, and any other custom attributes specific to your organization. Consider using a relational database such as SQL Server to store and manage employee data efficiently. Utilizing an ORM framework like Entity Framework can simplify the data access layer implementation and provide seamless integration with your application.

10.3.2 Employee Registration and Onboarding

The first step in managing employees is to provide a user-friendly interface for employee registration and onboarding. This feature allows HR personnel to enter new employee details into the system. The registration form should capture essential information such as name, contact details, address, and job-related details like department, position, and start date. Additionally, you can include features like document upload for identification and educational certificates, as well as an option to assign roles and permissions.

10.3.3 Employee Search and Filtering

As the number of employees grows, it becomes crucial to have an efficient search and filtering mechanism to locate specific employee records. Implementing a search functionality that allows HR personnel to search for employees based on various criteria such as name, department, position, or any custom attributes can significantly enhance productivity. Additionally, incorporating filters to narrow down search results based on specific attributes can further streamline the process.

10.3.4 Employee Performance Management

Performance management is a critical aspect of HR functions. Implementing a performance management module within your application can help track employee performance, set goals, and conduct performance reviews. This module should allow HR personnel to define performance metrics, assign goals to employees, and track their progress. Additionally, it should provide a mechanism for employees and managers to provide feedback and conduct performance evaluations.

10.3.5 Leave Management

Leave management is an essential HR function that involves tracking employee leaves, managing leave requests, and maintaining leave balances. Implementing a leave management module within your application can automate these processes and provide a centralized system for employees to request leaves and for HR personnel to approve or reject them. The module should also include features like leave balance calculation, leave accrual, and the ability to generate leave reports.

10.3.6 Employee Training and Development

Investing in employee training and development is crucial for the growth and success of any organization. Building a training and development module within your application can help HR personnel manage employee training programs, track training progress, and evaluate the effectiveness of training initiatives. This module should allow HR personnel to create training programs, assign employees to specific courses, track completion status, and generate reports on training effectiveness.

10.3.7 Employee Offboarding

When an employee leaves the organization, proper offboarding procedures need to be followed. Implementing an offboarding module within your application can help streamline this process and ensure that all necessary tasks are completed. This module should include features such as employee exit interviews, asset return tracking, and the ability to update employee records to reflect their departure.

10.3.8 Employee Self-Service Portal

Providing employees with a self-service portal can empower them to manage their own information and perform certain HR-related tasks independently. This portal can include features such as updating personal information, viewing pay stubs, submitting leave requests, and accessing training materials. Implementing a secure and user-friendly self-service portal can enhance employee satisfaction and reduce the administrative burden on HR personnel.

By incorporating these HR functions and employee management features into your C# and .NET business application, you can streamline HR processes, improve data accuracy, and enhance overall productivity within your organization. Remember to design the user interface with a focus on usability and provide comprehensive reporting capabilities to track and analyze HR-related data effectively.

10.4 Accounting and Financial Management

In any business, accounting and financial management are crucial aspects that require careful attention and precision. Building robust accounting and financial management features into your business application can greatly enhance its value and usability. This section will guide you through the process of designing and implementing these essential functionalities in your C# and .NET application.

10.4.1 Designing the Accounting System

Before diving into the implementation details, it is important to have a clear understanding of the accounting system's design. The design should align with generally accepted accounting principles (GAAP) and cater to the specific needs of your business. Here are some key considerations:

10.4.1.1 Chart of Accounts

The chart of accounts is the foundation of any accounting system. It defines the categories and subcategories used to classify financial transactions. Design a comprehensive chart of accounts that covers all relevant aspects of your business, such as revenue, expenses, assets, liabilities, and equity.

10.4.1.2 General Ledger

The general ledger is the central repository for all financial transactions. It records the debit and credit entries for each transaction and maintains the account balances. Design a robust general ledger that can handle the complexities of your business, including multiple currencies, accruals, and adjustments.

10.4.1.3 Financial Statements

Financial statements provide a snapshot of your business's financial health. Design the system to generate standard financial statements such as the balance sheet, income statement, and cash flow statement. Consider incorporating customizable reporting options to cater to specific reporting requirements.

10.4.1.4 Budgeting and Forecasting

Include features for budgeting and forecasting to help businesses plan and track their financial performance. Design the system to allow users to create budgets, compare actuals against budgets, and generate variance reports. Consider incorporating forecasting capabilities to project future financial outcomes based on historical data.

10.4.2 Implementing Accounting Functionality

Once you have a clear understanding of the accounting system's design, you can start implementing the accounting and financial management functionality in your C# and .NET application. Here are some key stcps to follow:

10.4.2.1 Chart of Accounts Management

Implement a user-friendly interface to manage the chart of accounts. Allow users to create, edit, and delete accounts and subaccounts. Provide validation to ensure the integrity of the chart of accounts and prevent duplicate or inconsistent entries.

10.4.2.2 General Ledger Transactions

Design a module to record financial transactions in the general ledger. Implement functionality to create journal entries, specifying the accounts to debit and credit, along with the corresponding amounts. Ensure proper validation and error handling to maintain data integrity.

10.4.2.3 Financial Statements Generation

Develop a reporting module that generates financial statements based on the recorded transactions. Implement algorithms to calculate account balances, perform necessary aggregations, and generate accurate financial statements. Consider providing options for different reporting periods, such as monthly, quarterly, and annual statements.

10.4.2.4 Budgeting and Forecasting

Build a module that allows users to create budgets, track actuals against budgets, and generate variance reports. Implement features to import historical data, perform calculations, and generate forecasts based on different scenarios. Ensure the system provides flexibility for users to customize budgeting and forecasting parameters.

10.4.2.5 Integration with Other Modules

Integrate the accounting and financial management functionality with other modules in your business application. For example, ensure that sales and purchase transactions automatically update the general ledger. Implement reconciliation features to match bank statements with recorded transactions. Consider integrating with payroll and HR modules to streamline financial reporting.

10.4.3 Ensuring Security and Compliance

Accounting and financial management involve sensitive and confidential data. It is crucial to implement robust security measures to protect this information. Here are some key considerations:

10.4.3.1 User Authentication and Authorization

Implement a secure user authentication system to ensure that only authorized users can access the accounting and financial management features. Use industry-standard authentication mechanisms, such as username/password or multi-factor authentication, to protect user accounts.

10.4.3.2 Role-Based Access Control

Implement role-based access control (RBAC) to define different levels of access and permissions for users based on their roles and responsibilities. Ensure that sensitive financial operations are restricted to authorized personnel only.

10.4.3.3 Data Encryption and Auditing

Implement encryption mechanisms to protect sensitive financial data both at rest and in transit. Use secure protocols and algorithms to encrypt data and ensure secure communication between the application and the database. Implement auditing features to track and monitor user activities for compliance purposes.

10.4.4 Testing and Validation

Thoroughly test the accounting and financial management functionality to ensure its accuracy and reliability. Implement unit tests to validate individual components and integration tests to verify the interaction between different modules. Perform end-to-end testing to simulate real-world scenarios and validate the system's behavior.

10.4.5 Conclusion

Building robust accounting and financial management features in your C# and .NET application requires careful planning, design, and implementation. By following the steps outlined in this section, you can create a powerful and secure accounting system that meets the specific needs of your business. Remember to adhere to accounting principles and ensure compliance with relevant regulations to maintain the integrity of your financial data.

11 - Building Robust and Secure Enterprise Apps

11.1 Designing for Scalability and Performance

Scalability and performance are crucial factors to consider when building enterprise applications. As your application grows and handles increasing amounts of data and user traffic, it is essential to ensure that it can handle the load efficiently and provide a seamless user experience. In this section, we will explore the best practices for designing your application to be scalable and performant.

11.1.1 Understanding Scalability

Scalability refers to the ability of an application to handle increasing workloads by adding resources or scaling horizontally. It is essential to design your application with scalability in mind from the beginning to accommodate future growth. Here are some key considerations for designing a scalable application:

11.1.1.1 Modular Architecture

A modular architecture allows you to break down your application into smaller, independent components. This approach enables you to scale individual components independently, adding more resources or replicating them as needed. By decoupling different parts of your application, you can distribute the workload and improve overall performance.

11.1.1.2 Load Balancing

Load balancing is a technique used to distribute incoming network traffic across multiple servers or resources. By implementing load balancing, you can ensure that no single server becomes overwhelmed with requests, improving both scalability and performance. Consider using load balancing techniques such as round-robin, least connections, or weighted distribution to evenly distribute the workload.

11.1.1.3 Caching

Caching is an effective way to improve application performance by storing frequently accessed data in memory. By caching data, you can reduce the number of database queries or expensive computations, resulting in faster response times. Consider using caching mechanisms such as in-memory caches or distributed caches to improve scalability and reduce the load on your backend systems.

11.1.1.4 Asynchronous Processing

Asynchronous processing allows your application to handle multiple requests concurrently, improving scalability and responsiveness. By offloading time-consuming tasks to background threads or queues, your application can continue to serve other requests without blocking. Consider using asynchronous programming techniques and message queues to handle long-running or resource-intensive operations.

11.1.2 Performance Optimization

In addition to scalability, optimizing the performance of your application is crucial for delivering a smooth user experience. Here are some best practices to consider when optimizing the performance of your enterprise application:

11.1.2.1 Database Optimization

Optimizing database performance is essential for improving the overall performance of your application. Consider the following techniques:

- Indexing: Properly indexing your database tables can significantly improve query performance. Identify frequently executed queries and create appropriate indexes to speed up data retrieval.
- Query Optimization: Analyze and optimize your database queries to ensure they are efficient and utilize the available indexes. Avoid unnecessary joins, use appropriate filtering conditions, and consider using stored procedures for complex queries.
- Connection Pooling: Implement connection pooling to reuse database connections, reducing the overhead of establishing new connections for each request.

11.1.2.2 Code Optimization

Optimizing your code can have a significant impact on the performance of your application. Consider the following techniques:

- Minimize Database Round Trips: Reduce the number of database round trips by fetching all required data in a single query or using techniques like eager loading or batch processing.
- Efficient Data Structures: Use appropriate data structures and algorithms to optimize memory usage and execution time. Consider using collections like dictionaries or hash sets for

fast data retrieval.

- Avoid Over-Engineering: Keep your codebase simple and avoid unnecessary abstractions or complex designs that can introduce performance overhead.

11.1.2.3 Caching and Data Access Optimization

Caching and optimizing data access can greatly improve the performance of your application. Consider the following techniques:

- Cache Data: Cache frequently accessed data to reduce the load on your backend systems. Implement cache invalidation strategies to ensure data consistency.
- Lazy Loading: Use lazy loading techniques to load data on-demand, reducing the initial load time of your application.
- Batch Processing: Optimize data access by using batch processing techniques to fetch or update multiple records in a single operation.

11.1.3 Performance Testing and Monitoring

To ensure that your application meets the performance requirements, it is essential to perform thorough performance testing and monitoring. Consider the following practices:

11.1.3.1 Load Testing

Perform load testing to simulate real-world scenarios and determine how your application performs under different levels of user traffic. Identify performance bottlenecks and make necessary optimizations to improve scalability and performance.

11.1.3.2 Performance Monitoring

Implement performance monitoring tools and techniques to continuously monitor the performance of your application in production. Monitor key metrics such as response times, CPU and memory usage, database query times, and network latency. Use this data to identify performance issues and make informed decisions for optimization.

11.1.3.3 Profiling

Use profiling tools to analyze the performance of your application and identify areas that require optimization. Profiling can help you pinpoint performance bottlenecks, such as slow database queries or CPU-intensive operations, and optimize them for better performance.

Conclusion

Designing for scalability and performance is crucial for building robust and efficient enterprise applications. By considering modular architecture, load balancing, caching, and asynchronous processing, you can ensure that your application can handle increasing workloads. Additionally, optimizing database access, code, and data retrieval, along with thorough performance testing and monitoring, will help you deliver a high-performing application.

11.2 Implementing Security Best Practices

Security is a critical aspect of building enterprise applications. In today's digital landscape, where cyber threats are constantly evolving, it is essential to implement robust security measures to protect sensitive data and ensure the integrity of your application. This section will guide you through the implementation of security best practices in your C# and .NET business applications.

11.2.1 Understanding Application Security

Before diving into the implementation of security measures, it is crucial to understand the importance of application security. Application security involves protecting your application from unauthorized access, data breaches, and other malicious activities. By implementing security best practices, you can safeguard your application and its data from potential threats.

There are several key aspects to consider when it comes to application security:

Authentication and Authorization

Authentication verifies the identity of users accessing your application, while authorization determines what actions they are allowed to perform. Implementing a robust authentication and authorization system ensures that only authorized users can access specific resources and perform authorized actions.

Data Security

Data security involves protecting sensitive data from unauthorized access, modification, or disclosure. This includes encrypting data at rest and in transit, implementing secure storage mechanisms, and following best practices for handling sensitive information.

Secure Coding Practices

Writing secure code is essential to prevent common vulnerabilities such as SQL injection, cross-site scripting (XSS), and cross-site request forgery (CSRF). By following secure coding practices, you can minimize the risk of introducing security vulnerabilities into your application.

Secure Communication

Secure communication ensures that data transmitted between your application and external systems is encrypted and protected from interception or tampering. This involves using secure protocols such as HTTPS and implementing proper certificate management.

11.2.2 Implementing Authentication and Authorization

Authentication and authorization are fundamental components of application security. In this section, we will explore how to implement these features in your C# and .NET business applications.

User Authentication

User authentication verifies the identity of users accessing your application. There are various authentication mechanisms available, such as username/password authentication, social login (OAuth), and multi-factor authentication (MFA). Depending on your application's requirements, you can choose the appropriate authentication method.

To implement user authentication in your C# and .NET application, you can leverage the built-in authentication features provided by the .NET framework, such as ASP.NET Identity or Azure Active Directory. These frameworks provide a robust foundation for managing user authentication, including features like password hashing, account lockout, and password reset.

User Authorization

User authorization determines what actions a user is allowed to perform within your application. It involves defining roles and permissions and associating them with specific resources or actions. By implementing user authorization, you can control access to sensitive functionality and data within your application.

In C# and .NET, you can implement user authorization using role-based or claims-based authorization. Role-based authorization assigns users to specific roles, and permissions are associated with these roles. Claims-based authorization, on the other hand, uses claims to define user attributes and permissions. You can choose the approach that best suits your application's requirements.

11.2.3 Protecting Data and APIs

Protecting data and APIs is crucial to ensure the security of your application. In this section, we will explore some best practices for securing data and APIs in your C# and .NET business applications.

Data Encryption

Encrypting sensitive data is essential to protect it from unauthorized access. You can use encryption algorithms such as AES (Advanced Encryption Standard) to encrypt data at rest and in transit.

Additionally, you should ensure that encryption keys are securely managed and protected.

Input Validation

Input validation is a critical security measure to prevent common vulnerabilities such as SQL injection and cross-site scripting. Always validate and sanitize user input to ensure that it meets the expected format and does not contain malicious code.

API Security

When building applications that consume or expose APIs, it is essential to implement proper security measures. This includes using secure communication protocols such as HTTPS, implementing API authentication and authorization mechanisms (e.g., API keys, OAuth), and validating and sanitizing API input.

11.2.4 Handling Concurrency and Transactions

Concurrency and transactions play a vital role in ensuring data integrity and consistency in enterprise applications. In this section, we will explore how to handle concurrency and transactions securely in your C# and .NET business applications.

Concurrency Control

Concurrency control is essential when multiple users or processes access and modify shared data simultaneously. Implementing proper concurrency control mechanisms, such as optimistic or pessimistic locking, helps prevent data inconsistencies and conflicts.

Transaction Management

Transactions ensure that a group of database operations is executed as a single unit of work. By implementing transactions, you can maintain data integrity and consistency, even in the presence of failures or concurrent access. Use the transaction management features provided by your database system or ORM framework to handle transactions securely.

11.2.5 Monitoring and Logging

Monitoring and logging are crucial for detecting and responding to security incidents and identifying potential vulnerabilities. In this section, we will explore how to implement monitoring and logging in your C# and .NET business applications.

Application Logging

Implementing proper application logging allows you to track and record important events and activities within your application. By logging relevant information, such as user actions, errors, and security-related events, you can gain insights into the application's behavior and detect potential security issues.

Security Monitoring

Implementing security monitoring mechanisms, such as intrusion detection systems (IDS) and security information and event management (SIEM) tools, helps you identify and respond to security incidents promptly. Monitor application logs, network traffic, and system events to detect and mitigate potential security threats.

Conclusion

Implementing security best practices is essential to building robust and secure enterprise applications. By understanding the importance of application security, implementing authentication and authorization, protecting data and APIs, handling concurrency and transactions securely, and implementing monitoring and logging, you can enhance the security of your C# and .NET business applications. Remember to stay updated with the latest security trends and regularly review and update your security measures to stay ahead of potential threats.

11.3 Handling Concurrency and Transactions

Concurrency and transactions are crucial aspects of building robust and secure enterprise applications. In a multi-user environment, it is essential to handle concurrent access to data to ensure data integrity and consistency. Transactions provide a mechanism to group multiple database operations into a single logical unit, ensuring that either all operations succeed or none of them do. This section will explore the concepts of concurrency and transactions and provide guidance on how to handle them effectively in your C# and .NET applications.

11.3.1 Understanding Concurrency

Concurrency occurs when multiple users or processes attempt to access and modify the same data simultaneously. Without proper handling, concurrency issues can lead to data inconsistencies and conflicts. It is crucial to identify potential concurrency problems and implement strategies to mitigate them.

Optimistic Concurrency Control

One approach to handling concurrency is optimistic concurrency control. In this approach, each user or process assumes that conflicts are unlikely to occur. When updating a record, the application checks if the record has been modified by another user since it was last retrieved. If no modifications are detected, the update proceeds. However, if changes are detected, the application can prompt the user to resolve the conflict.

To implement optimistic concurrency control, you can use techniques such as timestamp-based concurrency or comparing the original values of the record with the current values during the update operation. The .NET framework provides mechanisms to facilitate optimistic concurrency control, such as the RowVersion data type in Entity Framework.

Pessimistic Concurrency Control

Pessimistic concurrency control takes a more cautious approach by assuming that conflicts are likely to occur. In this approach, locks are acquired on the data to prevent other users or processes from modifying it until the lock is released. Pessimistic concurrency control ensures that only one user can access and modify the data at a time, eliminating the possibility of conflicts.

To implement pessimistic concurrency control, you can use techniques such as database locks or application-level locks. However, it is important to use locks judiciously to avoid performance degradation and potential deadlocks.

11.3.2 Managing Transactions

Transactions provide a way to group multiple database operations into a single logical unit. They ensure that either all operations within the transaction succeed, or none of them do. Transactions are essential for maintaining data integrity and consistency, especially when multiple operations need to be performed atomically.

ACID Properties

Transactions adhere to the ACID (Atomicity, Consistency, Isolation, Durability) properties, which define the characteristics of a reliable transaction:

- Atomicity: A transaction is treated as a single, indivisible unit of work. Either all operations within the transaction are committed, or none of them are. If any operation fails, the entire transaction is rolled back, and the database is left in its original state.
- Consistency: A transaction brings the database from one consistent state to another. The database must satisfy all defined integrity constraints before and after the transaction.
- Isolation: Each transaction is isolated from other concurrent transactions. The changes made by one transaction are not visible to other transactions until the changes are committed.
- Durability: Once a transaction is committed, its changes are permanent and survive any subsequent system failures.

Transaction Management in C# and .NET

C# and .NET provide robust support for managing transactions. The System.Transactions namespace in the .NET framework offers classes and interfaces to handle transactional operations. The TransactionScope class simplifies the management of transactions by providing a declarative programming model.

To use transactions in your C# and .NET applications, you can follow these steps:

1. Begin a new transaction using the TransactionScope class.
2. Perform database operations within the transaction scope.
3. Commit the transaction if all operations succeed, or roll back

the transaction if any operation fails.

4. Dispose of the transaction scope to release any resources associated with the transaction.

By using the TransactionScope class, you can ensure that all database operations within the scope participate in the same transaction. If an exception occurs, the transaction will be automatically rolled back, ensuring data consistency.

11.3.3 Handling Concurrency and Transactions Best Practices

To effectively handle concurrency and transactions in your enterprise applications, consider the following best practices:

- Identify potential concurrency issues early in the development process and design your data models and architecture accordingly.
- Use optimistic concurrency control whenever possible to minimize the impact on performance and user experience.
- Implement proper error handling and conflict resolution mechanisms to handle concurrency conflicts gracefully.
- Use transactions to group related database operations and ensure data integrity.
- Keep transactions as short as possible to minimize the impact on system performance and concurrency.
- Use the appropriate isolation level for your transactions to balance data consistency and concurrency.
- Monitor and log transactional activities to identify and resolve any issues promptly.
- Test your application thoroughly to ensure that concurrency and transaction handling work as expected under various scenarios.

By following these best practices, you can build robust and secure enterprise applications that handle concurrency and transactions effectively, ensuring data integrity and consistency.

Conclusion

Handling concurrency and transactions is crucial for building robust and secure enterprise applications. By understanding the concepts of concurrency and transactions and implementing best practices, you can ensure data integrity, consistency, and optimal performance in your C# and .NET applications.

11.4 Monitoring and Logging

Monitoring and logging are essential components of building robust and secure enterprise applications. They provide valuable insights into the health and performance of your application, help identify and diagnose issues, and enable you to make informed decisions for optimization and troubleshooting. In this section, we will explore the importance of monitoring and logging in enterprise apps and discuss various techniques and best practices for implementing them.

11.4.1 Importance of Monitoring

Monitoring your enterprise application is crucial for ensuring its availability, performance, and reliability. By monitoring key metrics and indicators, you can proactively identify and address potential issues before they impact your users and business operations. Here are some key reasons why monitoring is important:

1. **Performance Optimization**: Monitoring allows you to identify performance bottlenecks and optimize your application for better responsiveness and scalability. By tracking metrics such as response times, CPU and memory

usage, and database query performance, you can pinpoint areas that require optimization.

2. **Availability and Uptime**: Monitoring helps you ensure that your application is available and accessible to users. By monitoring server uptime, network connectivity, and application response times, you can detect and resolve issues that may cause downtime or service disruptions.

3. **Capacity Planning**: Monitoring enables you to plan for future growth and capacity requirements. By tracking resource utilization and user activity patterns, you can anticipate when additional resources or infrastructure upgrades may be needed.

4. **Security and Compliance**: Monitoring helps you detect and respond to security threats and vulnerabilities. By monitoring access logs, authentication attempts, and system events, you can identify suspicious activities and take appropriate measures to protect your application and data.

11.4.2 Logging Best Practices

Logging is the process of recording events, errors, and other relevant information during the execution of your application. It provides a valuable audit trail and helps in troubleshooting and debugging. Here are some best practices for implementing logging in your enterprise application:

1. **Use a Logging Framework**: Utilize a logging framework, such as log4net or NLog, to simplify the logging process and provide flexibility in configuring log levels, destinations, and formats. These frameworks offer features like log rotation, log filtering, and log aggregation.

2. **Log Important Events**: Log critical events, errors, and exceptions that occur during the execution of your

application. This information can be invaluable for diagnosing issues and understanding the root cause of failures.

3. **Include Contextual Information**: Include relevant contextual information in your log messages, such as timestamps, user IDs, request IDs, and session IDs. This additional information can help in correlating log entries and understanding the sequence of events leading to an issue.

4. **Log Levels**: Use different log levels (e.g., debug, info, warn, error, fatal) to categorize log messages based on their severity. This allows you to control the verbosity of your logs and filter out less critical information in production environments.

5. **Log Aggregation**: Consider using a centralized log aggregation tool, such as Elasticsearch, Logstash, and Kibana (ELK stack), or Splunk, to collect and analyze logs from multiple sources. This enables you to search, filter, and visualize log data, making it easier to identify patterns and trends.

6. **Log Retention and Rotation**: Define a log retention policy to manage the size and lifespan of your log files. Regularly rotate log files to prevent them from growing too large and consuming excessive disk space.

7. **Secure Logging**: Ensure that sensitive information, such as passwords or personally identifiable information (PII), is not logged in clear text. Use techniques like data masking or encryption to protect sensitive data in your logs.

11.4.3 Monitoring Techniques

Monitoring your enterprise application involves collecting and analyzing various metrics and indicators. Here are some common monitoring techniques and tools:

1. **Application Performance Monitoring (APM)**: APM tools,

such as New Relic or Application Insights, provide real-time insights into the performance and behavior of your application. They monitor metrics like response times, CPU and memory usage, database queries, and external service dependencies.

2. **Infrastructure Monitoring**: Monitor the health and performance of your infrastructure components, such as servers, network devices, and databases. Tools like Nagios, Zabbix, or Datadog can help you track resource utilization, network latency, and system availability.

3. **User Experience Monitoring**: Monitor the user experience by tracking metrics like page load times, error rates, and user interactions. Tools like Google Analytics or Pingdom can provide insights into user behavior and help identify usability issues.

4. **Log Monitoring**: Monitor your application logs in real-time to detect errors, exceptions, and other critical events. Tools like ELK stack, Splunk, or Graylog can help you aggregate, search, and analyze log data.

5. **Alerting and Notifications**: Configure alerts and notifications to proactively notify you when specific thresholds or conditions are met. This allows you to take immediate action and address potential issues before they impact your users.

11.4.4 Performance Monitoring and Optimization

Performance monitoring is crucial for ensuring that your enterprise application meets the required performance standards. Here are some techniques for monitoring and optimizing performance:

1. **Benchmarking**: Establish performance benchmarks and regularly measure your application's performance against

them. This helps you identify performance regressions and track the impact of optimizations.

2. **Profiling**: Use profiling tools, such as Visual Studio Profiler or JetBrains dotTrace, to identify performance bottlenecks in your code. Profiling helps you understand which parts of your application consume the most resources and need optimization.

3. **Caching**: Implement caching mechanisms, such as in-memory caching or distributed caching, to reduce the load on your application and improve response times. Monitor cache hit rates and adjust cache expiration policies based on usage patterns.

4. **Database Optimization**: Optimize database queries and indexes to improve database performance. Monitor slow queries and identify opportunities for query optimization or index tuning.

5. **Load Testing**: Conduct load testing to simulate real-world usage scenarios and identify performance limitations. Tools like Apache JMeter or Microsoft Azure Load Testing can help you simulate high user loads and measure application response times under stress.

By implementing effective monitoring and logging strategies, you can ensure the stability, performance, and security of your enterprise application. Regularly review and analyze the collected data to identify areas for improvement and take proactive measures to optimize your application's performance.

12 - Conclusion and Next Steps

12.1 Reviewing Key Concepts and Lessons Learned

In this book, we have covered a wide range of topics related to building business apps in C# and .NET. Throughout the chapters, we have explored various aspects of enterprise application development, from planning data models and architecture to deploying updates and managing versions. In this final section, we will review the key concepts and lessons learned throughout the book.

12.1.1 Understanding the Importance of Building Business Apps

In Chapter 1, we discussed the importance of building business apps and how they can streamline processes, improve efficiency, and enhance decision-making. We learned that business apps are essential tools for organizations to manage their operations effectively and gain a competitive edge in the market.

12.1.2 Overview of C# and .NET Framework

Chapter 1 also provided an overview of C# and the .NET Framework. We learned about the benefits of using C# as a programming language for building business apps, such as its simplicity, scalability, and extensive library support. Additionally, we explored the various components of the .NET Framework and how they contribute to the development process.

12.1.3 Planning Data Models and Architecture

In Chapter 1.3, we delved into the importance of planning data models and architecture. We discussed the significance of designing a robust and scalable data model that aligns with the business requirements. We also explored different architectural patterns, such as the layered architecture, and how they can be applied to build maintainable and extensible business apps.

12.1.4 Designing User Interfaces with Windows Forms

Chapter 1.4 focused on designing user interfaces with Windows Forms. We learned about the various controls and components available in Windows Forms and how to create visually appealing and user-friendly interfaces. We also discussed best practices for organizing and structuring the UI to enhance usability and productivity.

12.1.5 Working with Databases and ORM Frameworks

Chapter 2 introduced us to the world of databases and ORM frameworks. We explored SQL Server databases and learned how to create and manage databases effectively. We also discussed the benefits of using Entity Framework as an ORM framework for object-relational mapping, enabling us to work with databases in a more intuitive and efficient manner.

12.1.6 Implementing Business Logic and Validation

Chapter 3 focused on implementing business logic and validation. We discussed the importance of separating business logic from the presentation layer and explored various techniques for implementing business rules and workflows. Additionally, we learned how to validate user input and handle exceptions and errors gracefully.

12.1.7 Generating Reports in Business Apps

In Chapter 4, we explored the world of reporting in business apps. We learned about the RDLC format and how to use it for report design and generation. We also discussed the integration of third-party reporting libraries to enhance the reporting capabilities of our applications. Furthermore, we explored customization options and exporting reports in different formats.

12.1.8 Deploying Web-Based Apps to IIS

Chapter 5 focused on deploying web-based apps to IIS. We discussed the fundamentals of web-based applications and how to configure IIS for hosting these apps. We also learned about the process of publishing and deploying web apps and explored techniques for managing web app settings and security.

12.1.9 Securing Business Apps with Authentication/ Authorization

Chapter 6 delved into the critical aspect of securing business apps with authentication and authorization. We discussed the importance of app security and explored different techniques for implementing user authentication. Additionally, we learned how to manage user roles and permissions to control access to various parts of the application. We also discussed securing data and APIs to protect sensitive information.

12.1.10 Integrating with Web APIs

In Chapter 7, we explored the world of web APIs and integration. We discussed the fundamentals of web APIs and learned how to consume them in our business apps. We also explored techniques for handling API authentication and authorization and discussed best practices for working with API responses and error handling.

12.1.11 Testing and Debugging Best Practices

Chapter 8 focused on testing and debugging best practices. We discussed the importance of testing and debugging in ensuring the quality and reliability of our applications. We explored techniques for unit testing business logic and components and discussed various debugging techniques and tools. Additionally, we learned about performance testing and optimization to ensure our apps perform efficiently.

12.1.12 Deploying Updates and Managing Versions

Chapter 9 delved into the process of deploying updates and managing versions. We discussed the importance of deployment and versioning and explored techniques for implementing continuous integration and deployment. We also learned how to manage application versions and updates effectively and discussed rollback strategies and disaster recovery.

12.1.13 Building Common Business Features

Chapter 10 focused on building common business features. We explored various functionalities such as order processing and management, inventory management, HR functions, and accounting and financial management. We discussed the key considerations and best practices for implementing these features in our business apps.

12.1.14 Building Robust and Secure Enterprise Apps

Chapter 11 delved into building robust and secure enterprise apps. We discussed the importance of designing for scalability and performance and explored techniques for implementing security best practices. Additionally, we learned how to handle concurrency and transactions effectively and discussed the significance of monitoring and logging in maintaining the health and performance of our applications.

Conclusion

Throughout this book, we have covered a wide range of topics related to building business apps in C# and .NET. We have explored the key concepts and best practices for each aspect of enterprise application development, from planning and designing to deployment and maintenance. By following the step-by-step guide provided in this book, you will be well-equipped to build robust, secure, and efficient business apps that meet the needs of your organization.

Next Steps in Building Business Apps in C# and .NET

Now that you have completed this book, you may be wondering what your next steps should be in building business apps in C# and .NET. Here are a few suggestions to further enhance your skills and knowledge:

1. Stay updated with the latest advancements in C# and the .NET Framework by following relevant blogs, forums, and online communities.
2. Explore additional resources such as books, tutorials, and online courses that delve deeper into specific topics of interest.
3. Engage in practical projects to apply the concepts and techniques learned in this book to real-world scenarios.
4. Collaborate with other developers and participate in coding challenges or hackathons to enhance your problem-solving skills.
5. Continuously improve your understanding of software development principles and design patterns to build more maintainable and scalable applications.

Remember, building business apps is an ongoing learning process, and the more you practice and explore, the better you will become. Embrace new technologies, stay curious, and never stop learning. Good luck on your journey of building business apps in C# and .NET!

12.2 Exploring Further Resources

Congratulations on completing this comprehensive guide to building business apps in C# and .NET! By now, you should have a solid understanding of the key concepts and techniques involved in enterprise application development. However, the world of software development is constantly evolving, and there is always more to learn and explore. In this section, we will provide you with a list of further resources that can help you continue your journey and stay up-to-date with the latest trends and best practices in the field.

12.2.1 Online Learning Platforms

Online learning platforms offer a wide range of courses and tutorials that can help you deepen your knowledge and skills in C# and .NET development. Some popular platforms include:

- **Pluralsight**: Pluralsight offers a vast library of courses on various topics related to software development, including C# and .NET. Their courses are taught by industry experts and cover both beginner and advanced topics.
- **Udemy**: Udemy is another popular platform that offers a wide range of courses on C# and .NET development. They have courses for all skill levels, and many of them are created by experienced professionals.
- **LinkedIn Learning**: LinkedIn Learning (formerly Lynda.com) provides a vast collection of video courses on C# and .NET development. Their courses cover a wide range of topics, from beginner to advanced, and are taught by industry experts.

12.2.2 Books

Books are a great way to dive deeper into specific topics and gain a more comprehensive understanding of C# and .NET development. Here are some highly recommended books:

- **"C# in Depth" by Jon Skeet**: This book is a must-read for any C# developer looking to deepen their understanding of the language. It covers advanced topics and explores the intricacies of the C# language.
- **"Pro ASP.NET Core MVC" by Adam Freeman**: If you are interested in web development with ASP.NET Core MVC, this book is an excellent resource. It covers all aspects of building web applications using the MVC pattern.
- **"Entity Framework Core in Action" by Jon P. Smith**: This book provides a comprehensive guide to working with Entity Framework Core, including querying, data manipulation, and performance optimization.

12.2.3 Online Communities and Forums

Engaging with online communities and forums can be a valuable way to connect with other developers, ask questions, and learn from their experiences. Here are some popular online communities for C# and .NET developers:

- **Stack Overflow**: Stack Overflow is a question and answer site for programmers. It has a vast community of developers who are always ready to help with any coding-related questions.
- **Reddit**: Reddit has several communities dedicated to C# and .NET development, such as r/csharp and r/dotnet. These communities are great for discussing best practices, sharing

resources, and getting feedback on your projects.

- **Microsoft Developer Community**: The Microsoft Developer Community is an official forum for developers using Microsoft technologies. It is a great place to ask questions, find answers, and connect with other developers.

12.2.4 Blogs and Websites

Blogs and websites are excellent sources of information and tutorials on C# and .NET development. Here are some popular ones:

- **Scott Hanselman's Blog**: Scott Hanselman is a well-known developer and advocate for Microsoft technologies. His blog covers a wide range of topics, including C# and .NET development.
- **Telerik Developer Network**: The Telerik Developer Network provides a wealth of articles, tutorials, and resources on C# and .NET development. It covers various topics, including UI development, data access, and performance optimization.
- **Microsoft Docs**: Microsoft Docs is the official documentation site for Microsoft technologies, including C# and .NET. It provides comprehensive documentation, tutorials, and code samples to help you learn and master these technologies.

12.2.5 Open-Source Projects

Contributing to open-source projects is an excellent way to gain practical experience and collaborate with other developers. Here are some popular open-source projects related to C# and .NET:

- **ASP.NET Core**: ASP.NET Core is an open-source web framework for building modern web applications. Contributing to the ASP.NET Core project can help you gain a deeper understanding of web development with C# and .NET.
- **Entity Framework Core**: Entity Framework Core is an open-source ORM framework for .NET. Contributing to the Entity Framework Core project can help you understand the inner workings of the framework and contribute to its development.
- **.NET Core**: .NET Core is an open-source, cross-platform framework for building modern applications. Contributing to the .NET Core project can help you gain a deeper understanding of the framework and contribute to its development.

12.2.6 Conferences and Meetups

Attending conferences and meetups is a great way to network with other developers, learn from industry experts, and stay up-to-date with the latest trends in C# and .NET development. Some popular conferences and meetups include:

- **Microsoft Build**: Microsoft Build is an annual conference for developers focused on Microsoft technologies. It features keynotes, technical sessions, and hands-on workshops on various topics, including C# and .NET development.
- **.NET Conf**: .NET Conf is a free, virtual conference for developers using .NET technologies. It features live sessions, demos, and Q&A sessions with industry experts.
- **Local Meetups**: Many cities have local meetups dedicated

to C# and .NET development. These meetups provide an opportunity to connect with other developers in your area, learn from their experiences, and share your knowledge.

Remember, learning is a continuous process, and staying updated with the latest trends and best practices is crucial for your growth as a developer. Explore these resources, engage with the community, and continue building amazing business apps with C# and .NET!

12.3 Next Steps in Building Business Apps in C# and .NET

Congratulations on completing this comprehensive guide to building business apps in C# and .NET! By now, you have gained a solid understanding of the key concepts and techniques involved in developing enterprise applications. However, the journey doesn't end here. In this final section, we will explore the next steps you can take to further enhance your skills and continue building successful business apps.

12.3.1 Expand Your Knowledge with Advanced Topics

As you continue your journey in building business apps, it's essential to keep expanding your knowledge and staying up-to-date with the latest advancements in the field. Here are some advanced topics you can explore:

12.3.1.1 Cloud Computing and Microservices Architecture

Cloud computing has revolutionized the way applications are developed, deployed, and scaled. Explore cloud platforms like Microsoft Azure or Amazon Web Services (AWS) to understand how to leverage their services for building scalable and resilient applications. Additionally, delve into microservices architecture, which allows you to break down your application into smaller, independent services that can be developed, deployed, and scaled individually.

12.3.1.2 Machine Learning and Artificial Intelligence

Machine learning and artificial intelligence are transforming various industries. Consider learning about frameworks like TensorFlow or

Microsoft's Cognitive Services to incorporate intelligent features into your business apps. Explore topics such as natural language processing, computer vision, and predictive analytics to unlock the power of AI in your applications.

12.3.1.3 Mobile App Development

With the increasing popularity of mobile devices, it's crucial to have a strong presence in the mobile app market. Consider learning frameworks like Xamarin or React Native to build cross-platform mobile apps that can run on both iOS and Android devices. Understand the unique challenges and design considerations involved in mobile app development, such as responsive UI design and offline data synchronization.

12.3.2 Contribute to Open Source Projects

Contributing to open source projects is an excellent way to enhance your skills, collaborate with other developers, and give back to the community. Look for popular open source projects related to C# and .NET, such as ASP.NET Core or Entity Framework, and start contributing. You can fix bugs, add new features, or even create your own open source project. By participating in open source, you'll gain valuable experience and establish your reputation as a skilled developer.

12.3.3 Continuous Learning and Professional Development

Technology is constantly evolving, and it's crucial to stay updated with the latest trends and best practices. Here are some ways to continue your learning and professional development:

12.3.3.1 Attend Conferences and Workshops

Attend industry conferences and workshops related to C# and .NET development. These events provide opportunities to learn from industry experts, network with fellow developers, and gain insights into emerging technologies and trends. Look for conferences like Microsoft Build, .NET Conf, or local user group meetups.

12.3.3.2 Online Learning Platforms

Explore online learning platforms like Pluralsight, Udemy, or Coursera, which offer a wide range of courses on C# and .NET development. These platforms provide structured learning paths, allowing you to acquire new skills at your own pace. Additionally, consider joining online communities and forums to engage with other developers and seek guidance on specific topics.

12.3.3.3 Read Books and Technical Blogs

Books and technical blogs are excellent resources for deepening your understanding of specific topics. Look for books on advanced C# and .NET development, software architecture, design patterns, and best practices. Follow technical blogs and subscribe to newsletters to stay updated with the latest industry news and insights.

12.3.4 Build Real-World Projects

One of the most effective ways to solidify your skills and gain practical experience is by building real-world projects. Identify a problem or a business need and develop a solution using the concepts and techniques you have learned. This hands-on experience will not only enhance your technical skills but also provide you with valuable insights into the challenges and considerations involved in building business apps.

12.3.5 Collaborate with Other Developers

Collaboration is key to growth and learning as a developer. Engage with other developers through online communities, forums, or local meetups. Participate in code reviews, pair programming sessions, or hackathons. By collaborating with others, you can learn from their experiences, gain new perspectives, and improve your problem-solving skills.

12.3.6 Stay Updated with Frameworks and Tools

C# and .NET ecosystem is continuously evolving, with new frameworks, libraries, and tools being released regularly. Stay updated with the latest releases and enhancements to leverage the full potential of these technologies. Follow official documentation, blogs, and community forums to stay informed about new features, bug fixes, and best practices.

Conclusion

Building business apps in C# and .NET is an exciting and rewarding journey. By following this step-by-step guide, you have gained a solid foundation in developing enterprise applications. Remember to continue expanding your knowledge, contributing to the community, and building real-world projects to further enhance your skills. Embrace continuous learning and stay updated with the latest advancements in the field. With dedication and perseverance, you can become a proficient developer capable of building robust and successful business apps. Good luck on your future endeavors!